GREAT WAR LITERATURE

A-LEVEL STUDY GUIDE

Written by W Lawrance

on

BIRDSONG

A NOVEL BY SEBASTIAN FAULKS

Great War Literature A-Level Study Guide on Birdsong, a novel by Sebastian Faulks.
Written by W Lawrance

Published by:
Great War Literature Publishing LLP
Darrington Lodge, Springfield Road, Camberley, Surrey GU15 1AB Great Britain
Web site: www.greatwarliterature.co.uk
E-Mail: enquiries@greatwarliterature.co.uk

Produced in Great Britain

ISBN 978-1905378449 (1905378440) First Edition in Paperback - September 2008

10 9 8 7 6 5 4 3 2 1

Design and production by Great War Literature Publishing LLP
Typeset in Neue Helvetica, ITC Berkeley Old Style and Trajan Pro

Great War Literature A-Level Study Guide on

Birdsong

CONTENTS

Preface		5
Introduction		7
Synopsis		9
PartOne	- France 1910	9
Part Two	- France 1916	14
Part Three	- London 1978	22
Part Four	- France 1917	25
Part Five	- London 1978	32
Part Six	- France 1918	35
Part Seven	- England 1979	40
Character Analysis		43
1. Stephen Wraysford		43
2. Isabelle Azaire		51
3. Jack Firebrace		56
4. Michael Weir		59
5. Jeanne Fourmentier		62
6. Elizabeth Benson		65
Themes and Comparisons		67
1. Male Relationships		67
2. Portrayal of Love and Sex		72
3. Portrayal of the Home Front		78
4. The Depiction of Battle Scenes		82
Critical Analysis		87
1. The Structure of the Novel		87
2. Language		93
Historical Significance		97

Coursework Assistance   99
    1. Essay Suggestions   99
    2. Comparative Work   109
Further Reading   115
Bibliography   123
Other Titles   124

PREFACE

The primary purpose of Great War Literature Study Guides is to provide in-depth analysis of First World War literature for GCSE and A-Level students.

Great War Literature Publishing have taken the positive decision to produce a uniquely detailed and in-depth interpretation of selected works for students. We also actively promote the publication of our works in an electronic format via the Internet to give the broadest possible access.

Our publications can be used in isolation or in collaboration with other study guides. It is our aim to provide assistance with your understanding of First World War literature, not to provide the answers to specific questions. This approach provides the resources that allow the student the freedom to reach their own conclusions and express an independent viewpoint.

The structure of Great War Literature Study Guides allows the reader to delve into a required section easily without the need to read from beginning to end.

The Great War Literature Study Guides have been thoroughly researched and are the result of over 25 years of experience of studying this particular genre.

Studying literature is not about being right or wrong, it is entirely a matter of opinion. The secret to success is developing the ability to form these opinions and to deliver them succinctly and reinforce them with quotes and clear references from the text.

Great War Literature Study Guides help to extend your knowledge of First World War literature and offer clear definitions and guidance to enhance your studying. Our clear and simple layouts make the guides easy to access and understand.

The Great War Literature A-Level Study Guide on *Birdsong*, provides a critical assessment of many aspects of this novel and is based entirely on the opinion of the author of this guide.

INTRODUCTION

This book, initially published in 1993, has become a popular A-Level text, providing reasonable scope for coursework essays and discussion. The novel recounts the story of Stephen Wraysford. We follow him from his life as a young man in pre-war France, through the carnage of the trenches of the First World War. Stephen's passionate affair with Isabelle, the beautiful wife of his French host, and his despair when she abandons him, are contrasted with the desolation and slaughter of the front line trenches, which are evocatively brought to life.

Stephen and Isabelle discover love, but also find that sometimes love is not enough. Isabelle realises that security and stability can be more important than passion and excitement; while Stephen's experiences on the battlefield lead him, through extreme trauma, to a completely different type of love, born out of kindness and consideration.

Interwoven into this story is a modern section in which Elizabeth Benson attempts to trace her grandfather and discover his involvement in the First World War. This is an event in history of which she has little understanding and her journey leads her to discover the shocking truth of the slaughter on the battlefields of the Western Front.

One of the central themes to this story is man's ability to overcome adversity: to rise above his circumstances and survive - no matter what is thrown in his path. As Stephen learns this lesson, and finally pieces his life together, it would seem that the birds, which he has feared for so long, come to represent a soaring, singing freedom, and a will to live - typified in one word - *Birdsong*.

Percival George Waine
178th Tunnelling Company,
Royal Engineers.
*Image courtesy of gwpda.org and his
grandnephew, David Davies.*

Tunnellers

It has been estimated that in the First World
War there were over 20,000 men actively
engaged on each side, both attempting to
blow the other out of his trenches through
tunnelling.

It was Norton Griffiths, Conservative MP,
adventurer and businessman, who convinced
the military authorities that mining was a
realistic possibility in the Flanders mud, and a
priority if the army was not to be
"undermined" by the Germans.

There were many kilometres of tunnels, dug
by both sides, which ran under the muddy
battlefields, some with cavities the size of
quite large rooms filled with high explosives.

On occasion, tunnels would collide and in
this dark and claustrophobic environment,
sometimes 100 feet down, desparate hand-
to-hand fighting would take place.

*Source: War Underground: The Tunnellers of the
Great War by Alexander Barrie.*

BIRDSONG
BY SEBASTIAN FAULKS

SYNOPSIS

PART ONE - FRANCE 1910

The novel opens with the arrival of Stephen Wraysford in the Boulevard du Cange, at the home of René and Isabelle Azaire. Over the course of dinner, Stephen is also introduced to Lisette and Grégoire, the children of the house. Afterwards, they are joined by Monsieur and Madame Bérard, friends of the family, who stay and play cards. Stephen becomes aware of a certain tension between René and Isabelle which he does not at first understand. When he retires to bed, however, Stephen hears noises coming from another bedroom, and, upon investigation, it becomes clear that René Azaire is beating his wife.

Stephen visits Azaire's factory and meets Meyraux, the foreman and head of the syndicate, or union. Meyraux distrusts Stephen and the initial discussions between the union leader and the factory owner break down. Even while the two men are arguing, however, Stephen can only think of Isabelle Azaire. Later, alone in his room, Stephen notes his feelings for her in his coded notebook.

Over the coming days, amidst the whirl of work and engagements with the Bérards, Stephen has more time to study Isabelle. One afternoon, he strikes up a conversation with her, and, after learning that she is René's second wife and that Lisette and Grégoire are her stepchildren, he earnestly reassures her of his knowledge and understanding of her relationship with her husband. Isabelle, humiliated by this revelation and embarrassed by his remarks, remains aloof.

One day, while lunching alone in a café, Stephen notices Madame Azaire in the street outside. He leaves the café and catches up with her just as she is about to enter a small, drab apartment. She explains that she is bringing food to Lucien Lebrun, the leader of the dyers syndicate, for him to distribute amongst the needy families, who are struggling in the current industrial dispute. Stephen is uneasy about the familiarity between Isabelle and Lebrun and, upon leaving, he impulsively kisses her on the cheek.

We learn of Madame Azaire's childhood in a household of little affection. During her younger years, her sister, Jeanne, had been her sole companion and confidante. Following a disappointing romance with a young soldier named Jean Destournel (which had been broken up by her domineering father), Isabelle had become even more aloof and detached. Isabelle's father had introduced her to the widower, René Azaire, following which, she had agreed to marry him. Theirs had never been a relationship of love or passion; their love-making was performed with the sole intention of Isabelle becoming pregnant. Failure to achieve this had caused René to become bitter and angry: emotions which he took out on his wife.

As arranged, the following Sunday, the whole family join Monsieur and Madame Bérard on a boat-trip around the water-gardens in the upper reaches of the Somme River. The weather is hot and sultry and the extreme closeness of Isabelle in the small boat enhances Stephen's growing desire for his host's wife. These thoughts are intermingled with thoughts of death and decay brought on by the stagnant water and oppressive heat. Madame Azaire also seems aware of a physical tension between herself and Stephen, but retains her air of detached refinement.

The next morning Stephen receives a letter from his employers, summoning him back to London. He responds, saying that he needs at least one more month to complete his research thoroughly. He acknowledges to himself, however, that he also needs to resolve his feelings for Isabelle. He realises that he must act on his growing desire for her. At the factory the workers hold a meeting. A scuffle breaks out after someone suggests that Lucien Lebrun and Madame Azaire are friendlier than they should be. In the ensuing fight, Stephen manages to strike the man who had made the accusation, and feels gratified that he has struck a blow on behalf of Isabelle.

It is decided that, because of the disturbance at the factory, Stephen should stay at the Azaire's house for a few days, until the workers have calmed down again. The next day, Stephen joins Lisette and Isabelle for lunch, after which, they have coffee in the sitting room. Later, Lisette goes out into the garden. The sexual tension between Stephen and Isabelle is palpable and eventually he succumbs and kisses her. Initially she responds, but then rejects him and runs from the room. Stephen's desire for Isabelle is overwhelming and he finds it difficult to control himself. After a short while, however, she returns to the sitting room and tells him to follow her to the Red Room. Here they give in to their desires and make love passionately.

That evening, Stephen and Isabelle manage, with some difficulty, to hide their secret feelings from the rest of the family. The next day, he leaves the house, reluctant to remain under the same roof as Isabelle, while unable to be alone with her. He visits the local cathedral, where he is overcome by the sense that death is awaiting him and, indeed, the whole of his generation. Later, Stephen returns to the Boulevard du Cange desperate to find Isabelle. Everyone is out for the afternoon and they make love again. Afterwards they agree that, although they will keep their love a secret, they will find a way to exchange smiles and glances, unseen by the others, so that each will know that the other is happy. Isabelle explains her husband's violence: his inability to father another child has made him impotent and he hits her in the perverted hope that this will arouse him. Isabelle explains that she feels sorry for him because he humiliates himself, not her, by doing this. Stephen is angry that Azaire hurts Isabelle and begs her to forbid him from entering her room, although such an act is beyond her, as she fears his reactions.

The following weekend the whole family, plus Marguerite, the maid, go on a fishing trip. After lunch, Lisette finds Stephen alone and hidden from the others. She tells him that she knows about him and Isabelle and she wants him to make love to her too. He refuses, but she tries to seduce him and when he doesn't immediately pull away, she becomes frightened by the reality of the situation. Stephen manages to scare her into a promise of silence.

During the following week, Stephen and Isabelle are forced to snatch at opportunities for clandestine meetings as their passion shows no sign of abating. One afternoon, when they have made love again, Stephen and

Isabelle talk, for the first time, about their future and whether she will leave René and return to England with Stephen or whether he should remain in France with her.

René returns home from the factory, full of good news that the threatened strike has been averted. He also reveals that he has heard a rumour about his wife having an affair with Lebrun. She corrects him: her lover is not Lebrun, but Stephen. Stephen is surprised at this turn of events, but defends Isabelle, taking the blame for their affair upon himself. A bitter argument follows, and Isabelle and Stephen both pack their bags and leave.

They travel to the south and spend a few days resting in a hotel, before settling in a small rented house at St-Rémy-de-Provence. Stephen finds work as a carpenter's assistant and they begin their uncertain future together.

A few months later, Isabelle becomes aware that she is pregnant, but decides not to tell Stephen: she is beginning to have doubts about their relationship and their future. She is overjoyed at the prospect of having a child, but she is unsure how Stephen will react and how this will affect their lives together. In a letter to her sister, Jeanne, she reveals her doubts. She decides that what she and Stephen did was wrong and that she must spend some time away from him in order to decide what to do. She leaves, telling herself she will only stay with Jeanne for a few days, and then choose whether or not to return. When Stephen discovers her departure, he is broken: outwardly he continues as before, but inwardly he is hurt and confused and becomes cut-off from his own emotions.

Main Points of Interest in Part One

1. STEPHEN AND ISABELLE'S AFFAIR

- This is crucial to the construction of Stephen's character.
- Creates a passionate and heady atmosphere, which contrasts with the later parts of the novel.
- Isabelle becomes pregnant.

2. BUILDING CHARACTERS

- In particular that of Stephen Wraysford - the central character in the novel. We learn something about his childhood hardships and his outlook on life.
- The ending of the relationship between Isabelle and Stephen has a great impact on his character, although this does not become completely clear until later in the novel.
- Isabelle's sister Jeanne, who will go on to have a significant effect on Stephen later in the story, is introduced here as a compassionate and understanding person, who cares a great deal for her younger sibling.

3. INTRODUCTION OF FIRST WORLD WAR SETTINGS

- Sebastian Faulks makes good use of the settings which will later be involved in the First World War scenes, including Amiens, the Somme, Thiepval etc.
- Stephen and Isabelle's train journey after they leave the Boulevard du Cange, takes them on a route which mirrors that of the Western Front, mentioning many towns which would later become renowned as battlegrounds.

PART TWO - FRANCE 1916

We join Jack Firebrace, one of many tunnellers, digging out from the British front line trenches under No Man's Land. While working, the men hear a noise. Worried that it might be German tunnellers coming at them from the opposite direction, everyone stops digging and Jack, renowned for his good hearing, listens intently. After a while, he decides that the noise is shell-fire and they all go back to work. Moments later, there is an explosion and four men are killed. Later, Jack returns to the trenches, where he receives a letter from his wife, explaining that their son, John, is seriously ill in hospital. Jack goes on sentry duty, and while thinking about his son, he falls asleep. He is discovered by his commanding officer Captain Weir and an infantry Lieutenant, who tells Jack to report to him the following morning for punishment. Jack knows that if a court-martial finds him guilty of being asleep while on duty, the penalty is death by firing squad. He spends that night awake, wondering about his life and praying to God to spare him.

The next morning, Jack goes to the dugout as ordered and finds Captain Weir there with the other officer, Lieutenant Stephen Wraysford. Wraysford is in charge of an infantry platoon, but decides that he can take no action against Jack, since he is not in the same unit. Weir chooses not to pursue the matter either, so Jack's life is spared. As they talk, Jack wonders about Wraysford, who seems to have a strange outlook on life. When they talk about tunnelling, Wraysford tells Jack that he would like to go underground himself, to see what it is like.

The miners are relieved from duty and go back behind the lines to rest. They bathe, sleep, eat and drink at the local estaminet, sing songs and try to forget the war. Eventually, and with much dread, they return to the front line.

Back in the trenches, the infantry have been under fire for three days. Wraysford, whose nerves are beginning to fray, senses that his men are close to breaking point. He inspects the men and tries to make conversation with them, although he finds this difficult. One of the soldiers, Tipper, becomes overwhelmed by fear and loses control of himself, running down the trench, screaming. Wraysford is shocked by Tipper's reaction and orders that he be removed from the front line and taken back to the Medical Officer.

Later, Wraysford and Weir share a drink in Wraysford's dugout. They talk about the war to start with, but Weir is extremely nervous, so they start talking about women - just to change the subject. Weir confesses that he is a virgin and asks Wraysford whether he is sexually experienced. Eventually, Wraysford tells him something about Isabelle. While they are talking a shell explodes in the trench and Wraysford is summoned to help. He finds a scene of devastation, and spots the bodies of men to whom he had been talking that morning. He comes across a man named Douglas, who is bleeding heavily. Stephen sits down and speaks to him, trying to offer reassurance that he will be alright. After Douglas has been loaded onto a stretcher, another shell explodes and Stephen is blown into the air. He lands unharmed, but sees that one of the stretcher-bearers has been hit and that Douglas has been tipped over onto the floor of the trench. Covered in Douglas's blood, Wraysford is overwhelmed by panic.

Stephen's company is relieved and they go for three days rest to Béthune. Once he has slept, Stephen sits and reminisces about his days in pre-war France; about Isabelle, their passionate affair and his reaction to her sudden departure; his arrival in Paris and platonic friendship with Mathilde, a neighbour's daughter. He remembers also, how on the outbreak of war, he had travelled back to London and, along with countless others, eagerly enlisted, believing that the war would soon be over. At breakfast, Wraysford and Captain Gray discuss Wraysford's platoon and his feelings towards his men. They also talk about Weir and the tunnellers.

Back in the trenches, Wraysford is ordered by Captain Gray to gather volunteers to go down into the tunnel to provide fighting support for the tunnellers. [The idea being that if the Germans break through into the British tunnel, or vice versa, the men who are digging need armed infantry support]. Wraysford and his men, Byrne and Hunt, are joined by Jack Firebrace and descend the ladder to the tunnel. Jack takes them to the fighting tunnel, but after only a short time, the Germans break through. A fight ensues, during which Stephen is wounded. His limp body is dragged back to the surface. Upon arrival there, however, they find there has been heavy shelling and tending to Wraysford's wounded neck and shoulder is not a priority. By the time a stretcher-bearer takes him back to the dressing station, fever and infection have taken hold. He becomes delirious, remembering his childhood and Isabelle. Slowly but surely, Stephen feels that his life is slipping away.

Later, a concerned Jack goes back down to the dressing station to find out what happened. He is told that Stephen is dead and his body has been put with all the other corpses. Jack decides to go and say a prayer over his dead body, but when he gets there, he finds that Wraysford is still alive, surrounded by mutilated and rotting corpses.

Captain Weir, meanwhile, is worried because he has heard nothing from, or about, Wraysford. He starts to think that Stephen must be dead and tries to imagine life without his friend. He becomes very emotional and concludes that if Stephen is dead, he will try to get himself killed too.

Stephen is in hospital. Having been rescued by Jack, he is now recovering quite quickly from his injuries: the infection has cleared up and he's on the mend. He witnesses the plight of other men who come into the ward with terrible injuries. He is told that he will be able to leave the hospital at the end of the week, having spent twenty days there. Captain Gray visits him and tells him he can have two weeks leave and a promotion, after which he can take a job at headquarters. Wraysford refuses all of this and asks Gray to let him stay in the trenches. Grey tells him that they are going to be transferred to Auchonvillers, to attack the Germans and draw the fire away from the French at Verdun. Despite this, Stephen still prefers to remain with his men and face the forthcoming battle. Gray agrees to speak to their senior officer to have the orders reversed.

Fully recovered and back in the dugout, Wraysford and Weir discuss their forthcoming move to new trenches and Wraysford hints that he has planned a surprise for Weir before they depart. Weir has heard rumours that this surprise might involve the loss of his virginity to a local farm girl and he is terrified. Meanwhile, Jack has received another letter from his wife, but he fears opening it, in case it contains are bad news about his son.

Stephen takes Weir to the infamous farmhouse. Weir goes into a bedroom with the farm girl's mother, but returns a little later, clearly upset. Stephen panics, unsure as to what exactly has taken place and goes to make sure that the woman is alright. When he finds her, she says that Weir had begun to cry as soon as she had touched him. She decides she wants Stephen instead, but he says he will only have sex with the woman's daughter. He undresses, but is unable to proceed as his mind fills with thoughts, firstly of Isabelle and their shared passion, then of the shattered and broken bodies of men. In this state of confusion, he takes out his knife and presses it against the girl's skin. She is afraid, but he relents and she shows him more kindness and generosity than he believes he deserves. Weir and Wraysford return to their respective companies to find that they have not been missed. Neither of them mentions the farmhouse, or what took place there.

Finally, Jack reads the letter from his wife. She informs him that their son, John, has died and hopes that Jack will return home safely to her. Jack wants to pray to God and give thanks for his son's life, but finds that he is overcome by grief and simply weeps.

The division move to Albert and preparations begin for the Battle of the Somme. Wraysford and Gray are summoned to see Colonel Barclay who is interested to hear about the local area from Stephen. They enjoy a fine lunch with the Colonel and several other officers, before returning to their company.

The bombardment that precedes the forthcoming battle commences, and Stephen and his men march up towards the front line. Upon arrival, he meets with Weir, who tells him that his men have set the charges for a massive explosion due to go off just before the infantry go over the top. Later, after a communion service, the men are informed that the attack has been postponed for two days. Gray and Wraysford talk and Stephen learns that the German wires have not been cut and they are in for a fierce and bloody battle. The delay gives the men time to write letters home. Stephen writes to

Isabelle, although he believes she will never read his letter. He tells her how frightened he is and that he has always loved her. Jack writes lovingly to his wife and tells her that, although he is terribly sad about John's death, they must have faith in God and be thankful to Him for John's life.

That night, the men cannot sleep as they wait for the battle to begin. The barrage intensifies and they learn that they will go over the top at 7.30am - in daylight. At 7.20, a mine explodes, but still, they must wait ten minutes more. Finally, they start. Stephen crosses No Man's Land. It is hell - men fall all around him and, despite stumbling himself, he miraculously finds a gap in the wire and falls into an unmanned German trench. Initially he cannot decide what to do - he is completely alone and unsure whether to advance or retreat. Eventually he chooses to press on with the attack and finds himself in a shell-hole with six men from another regiment. All his own men would appear to be dead. One man in the shell-hole is very badly wounded and begs Stephen to shoot him, which he does.

Jack and a fellow tunneller, Arthur Shaw, witness the carnage from an elevated position behind the British trenches. They are joined by the padré, Horrocks, who initially offers prayers and words of comfort. As they see more and more groups of men leave the trenches to be mown down by a hail of bullets, Arthur Shaw breaks down and weeps, Horrocks throws away his silver cross in disgust at the waste of human lives and Jack realises that his faith in God has died.

Back in his shell-hole, Stephen sees that any attempt to move forward from his position is futile, so he risks his life and runs backwards towards the Ancre River, where, eventually, he finds water into which he submerges himself. Weakened and exhausted, he is carried away by the current of the river and is suddenly surrounded by German prisoners. They are all trying to escape from the rushing water but only Stephen is plucked to safety by an unknown British Private. The Germans are left to their fate. Stephen decides that he should try to continue the advance and sets off towards the German lines, only to be wounded. Lying in a shell-hole, he wakes to find Tyson, one of the tunnellers, who has been volunteered as a stretcher-bearer, dressing his wounds. Tyson tells Stephen that his wound is not serious and promises to send Weir to him. Over three-quarters of the men in Stephen's battalion have been killed.

Weir finds Stephen in his shell-hole and together they wait for darkness to fall. As it does, they realise how many wounded men there are - initially because the earth itself seems to be moving as the wounded crawl back to their own trenches; but then they hear the moaning sounds of men who cannot move and are calling for help. Weir becomes almost hysterical with fear, so Stephen cradles and comforts him.

Main Points of Interest in Part Two

1. INTRODUCTION OF THE WAR
- This is, essentially, the whole point of the novel.
- We learn how and why Stephen joined the army and the effect which his failed relationship with Isabelle had on this decision.
- The geographical area in which the first part of the novel had been set, features greatly in part two - providing Stephen with even less opportunity to forget Isabelle.

2. CONTINUING TO INTRODUCE AND BUILD CHARACTERS
- We are introduced to many new characters, including the influential Michael Weir and Jack Firebrace.
- The backgrounds and upbringing of these characters are given, so that the reader can better understand their actions and reactions to the war.

3. THE WAR BEGINS TO AFFECT CERTAIN INDIVIDUALS
- Jack Firebrace, upon witnessing the slaughter on the Somme battlefield, loses his faith in God.
- Michael Weir, already a nervous individual, becomes more and more easily agitated and dependent on Stephen and alcohol.
- Stephen becomes progressively more attached to his men and some of his fellow officers - an emotional connection which he had originally felt reluctant to embrace.

4. STEPHEN IS WOUNDED
- Stephen's wounds, received during the underground fighting, cause Weir to reassess their friendship.
- A link between Jack Firebrace and Stephen is formed, which will have a great impact later in the story.

5. THE BATTLE OF THE SOMME

- Many of the minor characters are killed during this action, which demonstrates the transient nature of some of the friendships formed during the conflict.

- We are made aware that some of the men killed are extremely young and inexperienced, which forces the reader to reassess Stephen's life: he is only 26 himself - although he seems much older.

- The letters written immediately before the battle reveal a great deal about the characters involved. They also force us to become more attached to each individual, thus making their deaths more significant.

PART THREE - LONDON 1978

Elizabeth Benson, a single, independent woman of 38, returns from a business trip to Germany. She receives an apologetic letter from her married lover, Robert, and goes out to dinner with some friends. The next afternoon, she goes to visit her mother, Françoise. She sees a familiar photograph of herself and her grandmother, taken when she was three years old, and her curiosity is aroused. Elizabeth enquires about her grandfather, of whom she knows nothing. Her mother seems vague, but says that she may have some papers of his in her attic. Elizabeth decides that, starting with these records, she will track down this man, to discover who he was and, hopefully, more about herself.

At work, she quizzes her older colleagues, Erich and Irene about their knowledge of the First World War, but learns nothing - they don't like to dwell on something so morbid. Irene, however, suggests that Elizabeth might like to talk to her husband, Bob.

Elizabeth drives through northern France, en-route to visit Robert in Brussels. She stays at a small hotel in Arras. The next day, she drives towards Albert, stopping at the Thiepval Memorial, which she has spotted from the road. Here, talking to the caretaker, she discovers that the thousands of names which cover the walls are just the *missing* from the adjacent fields. She is shocked by the number of dead.

She drives on to see Robert in Brussels. They spend the weekend together and, just before leaving, she raises the topic of marriage. He says he cannot bear to leave his daughter. Elizabeth explains that she is not prepared to wait forever - she wants a child herself, and that need is not going to go away. Robert suggests that Elizabeth should find someone else who is free to marry her and give her children. She replies that such an idea is impossible: she loves Robert and wants *his* children. There seems to be no possible compromise and they part with an uneasy atmosphere between them.

When she returns to England, Elizabeth goes to visit her mother and looks through some old boxes in the attic. She finds several items, including a coded notebook, which seem to date from the First World War and bear the name of her grandfather, Stephen Wraysford. Once again, she asks Françoise about her grandfather and Françoise says simply that he would have loved Elizabeth. She takes Stephen's notebook to the house of her colleague, Irene, whose husband, Bob, knows a lot about languages and codes, in the hope that he can translate the contents. Bob agrees that he will try to decode the notebook.

Elizabeth has a date with Stuart - a man to whom she had been introduced by her match-making friends. Their date is interesting, but it sets Elizabeth wondering why she continues to see Robert. Eventually she begins to understand that it might be because there is a strange freedom attached to seeing a married man, which allows her to continue to live her own life.

Main Points of Interest in Part Three

1. THE 'MODERN' SECTION

- Essentially, a narrative instrument, used to fill in the gaps in the story which would make the war-time element of the story too long-winded and clumsy.

2. CHARACTERS

- Although there is a little initial confusion as to who Elizabeth Benson is, it soon becomes clear that she is Stephen's granddaughter. Her grandmother, at this stage, is assumed to be Jeanne.
- Elizabeth's relationship with Robert, to a certain extent, mirrors the one between Isabelle and Stephen.

3. COMPLACENCY

- Elizabeth's journey to discover more about her grandfather, demonstrates her ignorance on the subject of the First World War.
- Other characters are shown as complacent or dismissive of the First World War, showing how easily it has been forgotten.

PART FOUR - FRANCE 1917

Stephen and his company are back in their old pre-Somme sector, manning the front-line trenches in Flanders. He has been made Company Commander; Gray is now Battalion Commander; the other Platoon Commander, Harrington, lost a leg on the Somme and has gone home. Most of the men around him now are strangers, but Stephen is happy to renew his friendship with Weir, who seems to rely increasingly on whisky, and has become even more nervous than he was before.

We learn that during his leave in England in October 1916, Weir had found that nothing had changed at home, except that he no longer belonged there. His father seemed to think that he knew all about the realities of the war just from the newspaper reports and wasn't interested in hearing his son's explanations.

Back in France, and reunited with his old friend, Weir asks Stephen to tell his fortune. Both men are drunk, but Stephen agrees. Afterwards, Weir, Stephen and Ellis (a young subaltern) discuss their feelings about the war. Weir is very bitter about the complacency of those at home; Ellis is naive enough to still be full of patriotic fervour. Stephen says the only loyalty he now feels is towards his dead comrades.

Jack Firebrace writes a letter to his wife. He tells her what he is doing and reveals that he is still haunted by John's death. He attends church services, but cannot find the enthusiasm for life and happiness which he used to have.

The Germans explode one of their mines, causing one of the British tunnels to collapse. Weir and Wraysford go underground to see if either of the men in the tunnel have survived. They take a canary with them to give them advance warning of gas. Finding that the tunnel has completely given way, they realise that the tunnellers must be dead. There is another minor collapse and Weir's arm is broken. Stephen must overcome his fear of birds, take the canary they brought underground with them, and lead his injured friend back to the surface.

Stephen and Ellis are granted permission to go to Amiens on leave. Stephen is, initially, unsure whether he wants to revisit the place where he and Isabelle first began their affair, but decides to go anyway. When they get to the town, they visit a bar but Stephen cannot relax amongst the other soldiers and leaves to find somewhere less busy - where the locals drink. Here, he comes across Jeanne, Isabelle's sister, and follows her outside, desperate to discover Isabelle's whereabouts. Reluctantly, Jeanne tells him that their father had persuaded Azaire to take Isabelle back and, encouraged by Grégoire, she had resumed her life in the Boulevard du Cange. On the outbreak of war, Azaire, with most of the other men, had been deported to Germany. Lisette had married, so Isabelle moved to a smaller apartment. This had been hit by a shell and Isabelle had been injured. Jeanne had come to Amiens to help her sister while she recovered. Stephen begs Jeanne to let him meet Isabelle. She refuses, but eventually agrees to tell Isabelle of his presence in the town, and let her make her own decision.

The next evening, Stephen again meets Jeanne to find that Isabelle has agreed to see him. They walk together to the house which Isabelle and Jeanne share. Noticing her scarred features, he initially finds it difficult to speak and is almost overwhelmed by emotion, but after a while, he becomes more calm and she tells him about her life since they last met.

In her story, she recounts her reconciliation with Azaire, the beginning of the war and her husband's bravery when he was deported. She also tells Stephen of the German occupation and how a young Prussian, named Max, had looked after her and she had fallen in love with him. She reveals that she received the letter which Stephen wrote on the eve of the Battle of the Somme and was full of anguish, knowing that Max was also in the same sector. The one thing she keeps from him is the birth of his daughter. Unaware even of her existence, Stephen leaves Isabelle, outwardly full of generous good wishes for her future with Max.

When Stephen returns to his battalion, he goes to see Colonel Gray, who tells him he must take some rest. He orders Stephen to have a spell of leave England followed by a 'staff' job of two or three months as an interpreter at Headquarters. Stephen's reluctance is obvious, but Gray is insistent. He has noticed that Stephen is tired - not just physically but that his emotions seem to be shattered too.

Jeanne becomes Stephen's companion when he is on leave. She is worried by his apathy, but encourages him to have hope. She believes that he will survive and tells him that she will wait for him.

Main Points of Interest in Part Four

1. STEPHEN MEETS JEANNE

- Isabelle's sister has only been a background character until now.
- Stephen's meeting with her begins their own friendship and provides a link with his past.
- Their friendship continues to flourish.

2. MEETING WITH ISABELLE

- The reader is made aware of the existence of Stephen's daughter - although he is kept in the dark.
- Isabelle wants to move on from her relationship with Stephen, despite her continued physical attraction to him.
- Stephen finally begins the slow process of accepting that Isabelle's place in his life is firmly in the past.

3. ISABELLE LEAVES FRANCE

- Following the wounding of her German lover, Max, Isabelle leaves France for good, knowing that she can never return.
- This action forces Stephen to accept that she does not love him anymore. This allows him to focus more on Jeanne and his friendship with her.

4. LEAVE IN ENGLAND

- Stephen's exhaustion leads to him being granted leave in England.
- While there, he finds it hard to relax, until he manages to find peace and a sense of unity with nature.
- Realising this new-found hope makes him more reluctant than ever before, to return the trenches.

5. WEIR'S DEATH

- Just before Stephen is due to lead the raid, he becomes angry with Weir and pushes him to the ground.
- Before the two men are able to meet again, Weir is killed.
- Stephen's grief takes the form of a breakdown. He simply ceases to function and is only saved by the intervention of Colonel Gray.

6. OTHER SIGNIFICANT DEATHS

- Ellis is machine gunned during the attack on the canal.
- Jack's particular friend, Arthur Shaw is killed when the tunnel collapses.
- Brennan finds the dismembered and rotting body of his brother in No Man's Land and brings him back to the trenches for a proper burial.

PART FIVE - LONDON 1978

Elizabeth is still on the trail of her grandfather. His notebook is proving difficult to translate, so she goes to the Headquarters of his old regiment where she is allowed to look at the Regimental History. This reveals the name of Colonel Gray. Elizabeth discovers his whereabouts and telephones him. He obviously remembers Stephen Wraysford and manages to give her a few details. His wife, cutting the conversation short, due to her husband's fatigue, suggests she try contacting a man named Brennan.

Elizabeth finds Brennan in a Star and Garter Home in Southend. She is shocked to discover that he has been living there for nearly sixty years. He suffered from shell-shock and had a leg amputated right at the end of the war: he now lives in a world of his own, untouched by reality. She manages to understand a few snippets of information from his almost incoherent ramblings and eventually leaves, overwhelmed by pity for this broken man.

Robert finds himself unexpectedly in London and Elizabeth spends the night with him at his flat. For once, they are both relaxed, neither of them mention his marriage or their future.

That Saturday, Françoise calls to say she has found more of her father's notebooks. Elizabeth collects them and goes back to her flat to read, completely forgetting that she has invited Stuart round for dinner. She resents his intrusion, but manages to concoct a meal, after which he proposes marriage, in a somewhat pompous and unconventional manner. Although she has already decided against him, she promises, not very truthfully, to think about his offer.

After the new year, Elizabeth goes to visit Tom Brennan again. She has decided to keep visiting him, not for information, but because she feels she owes it to him and his generation to show that she cares. On this second visit, she does not learn anything new about her grandfather, as Brennan merely repeats everything he has already told her.

Elizabeth discovers that she is pregnant. Although she is initially unsure as to how she feels about this, she gradually warms to the idea and is soon excited at the prospect of motherhood. She tells Robert, whose reaction is confused, but supportive.

She hears from Irene's husband, Bob, that he has managed to translate Stephen's 1918 notebook and he sends her a couple of pages. On reading it, she is transported to a sixty-year old world of waste, desolation, despair and utter, utter hopelessness.

Main Points of Interest in Part Five

1. ELIZABETH CONTACTS GRAY AND BRENNAN

- The discovery of these two survivors provides Elizabeth with the first tangible link to her grandfather

- We learn that Brennan believed Stephen to be 'mad', while Gray remembers him as 'strange', but a 'tremendous fighter'.

- Brennan's sad condition contrasts with his earlier contentment at finding his brother's rotting, dismembered corpse and bringing it back to the trenches for burial.

2. ELIZABETH DISCOVERS SHE IS PREGNANT

- Despite her protestations to her friends that she is not bothered about motherhood, Elizabeth is elated to discover that she is pregnant.

- This event puts her relationship with Robert in a completely different context.

3. STEPHEN'S NOTEBOOKS ARE TRANSLATED

- As well as discovering that there is more than one notebook, Elizabeth is also able to read them, as Bob has managed to complete the translation of the first book.

- The small excerpt given shows that Stephen's mind and existence have become tortured. He is haunted by what he has seen and done and can see no hope for his generation. He believes that, even those who survive will be forever disconnected from the rest of the world.

PART SIX - FRANCE 1918

As we rejoin Stephen, he is still doing his staff job and has just finished making an entry in his notebook. The next day he goes to Battalion Headquarters and Gray tells him that he is being sent back to his old company in the trenches, to take part in the final push into Germany. Stephen is not worried about this news - he no longer feels anything. Life has changed for the tunnellers. They are no longer required to dig and spend their time mending roads instead. Jack seems less happy than most of his comrades at this change in circumstances.

Before rejoining his Company, Stephen visits Jeanne, who has moved to Rouen following the German advance that spring. She can hardly fail to notice the physical and mental alteration in Stephen, but she tries to cheer him up. During one conversation, she tells him that Isabelle is happily settled with Max, who has had a leg amputated. He wonders why Jeanne is so kind to him and she reveals that she loves him and simply wants to have the opportunity to make their lives better. Later, they talk, lightheartedly about the future. When they go to bed, Stephen accidentally walks into her bedroom, while looking for the bathroom. He finds her naked and she beckons him to come nearer. She holds him to her and he begins to weep like a child, calling her sister's name.

Stephen returns to the front line trenches, and agrees that the next day, he will inspect a tunnel which runs out into No Man's Land. While in the tunnel, there is an explosion. Stephen's arm is hurt, but otherwise he is unharmed. Initially, he thinks he is the only man to have survived and contemplates retracing his steps to the surface. Then he becomes aware that someone else is moving nearby, so he starts to dig. The trapped man is Jack Firebrace. Stephen manages to clear away most of the earth around him, but Jack's legs are buried under some debris. Another explosion goes off behind them, which means that there may be no way for them to get out. Eventually, Jack is freed, but is very badly injured and Stephen must carry him back through the tunnel. Stopping en-route to check that no-one else is still alive, they finally reach a dead-end: the second explosion has blocked the tunnel and they are trapped. In the darkness, waiting for their inevitable deaths, Stephen and Jack talk. Jack, for the first time, openly confesses his deep feelings of loss over the death of his son; he tells Stephen how much he loved his little boy and the deep impact John has had on his life. Stephen talks, very briefly, about Isabelle. Jack admits that he does not anticipate getting out of the tunnel alive, and even if he does, his wife is too old to have another child, so Stephen promises that, if he survives, he will have children on Jack's behalf.

The two men decide that they must find a way out of the tunnel. Stephen picks Jack up again and they go back the way they came. They branch off into a side tunnel, where they pass the bodies of Jack's colleagues. Eventually, however, they can go no further. Jack has become too much of a burden for Stephen, so he leaves him propped up against the side of the tunnel and goes to find a separate space where he can be alone. Both men drift in and out of sleep and consciousness. When Stephen awakes he finds that he is lying close to a wall of sandbags. Confused, he returns to Jack, who explains that this could indicate the presence of explosives. Stephen becomes more optimistic - they could blow up the explosives and free themselves. After hours of clearing away the sandbags, Stephen finds himself in a chamber containing a vast quantity of explosives. In his brief moments of lucidity, Jack explains that if they blow up all of these, they will be blown up too. Stephen must clear most of the boxes back down the tunnel, before setting off an explosion. In his weakened state, this takes him days to accomplish. Finally, however, it is done and he manages to explode what is left in the chamber.

In the German trenches, a young German-Jewish doctor, named Levi, is startled by the force of the explosion. He and two other men, Lamm and Kroger, are sent down the tunnel to rescue the German miners, who entered it only minutes before. Levi is worried that one of the trapped men may be his younger brother, Joseph. The three Germans reach a blockage in the tunnel which despite hours of digging, they are unable to move. They use a small charge and try to blow their way through.

Despite the explosion, Stephen and Jack are still buried, but they hear the small German detonation and Stephen hopes that it is a rescue party. He talks to Jack, trying to keep him alive. He speaks openly of Isabelle and how his meeting her has changed his life. As he talks, Jack starts to choke and Stephen cradles him while they wait for their rescuers.

One of the German rescuers discovers the body of Levi's brother, Joseph. Lamm and Kroger are reluctant to continue further into the unstable tunnels, but Levi persuades them that his brother is not the only soldier who deserves a proper burial, so they continue to dig.

Meanwhile, Stephen and Jack take turns placing their mouths against the tiny air hole made by their explosion and in their moments of conversation, Jack seems more lucid than previously. Stephen hears the rescuers working in the distance, but as he begins to talk of freedom, Jack protests that he would rather not live any longer. He takes one final breath and dies, leaving Stephen alone. Tapping loudly with his knife on the chalk surface next to his head, Stephen waits in the darkness, hoping that his rescuers will get to him in time.

Levi hears the tapping sound and urges his colleagues to use another charge in order to free the obviously trapped man. Kroger points out that they may not, in fact, be rescuing a fellow German, but one of the British miners. Although Levi believes this is unlikely, he still thinks that they should continue, even though it would mean they were risking their own lives to save someone who had been responsible for his brother's death. The charge is exploded and the tapping sound is now much closer. Levi is excited - there is just a small amount of earth to be cleared and they will be able to reach whoever is trapped.

Stephen feels the explosion and initially panics that he will be buried alive. He begins to wonder who has been sent to rescue him - believing that it is British tunnellers who are approaching. He thinks of the world outside: of Jeanne and the continuation of his life. His desperation to survive suddenly becomes overwhelming.

After hours of digging, much of it with their bare hands, Levi is the first of the Germans to enter Stephen's tomb. When Stephen realises that his rescuers are, in fact, the enemy, his initial reaction is to fight, but then despite his impulses, he finds himself hugging Levi, the man whose brother he had killed.

When they return to the surface, the German trench is empty. Looking through binoculars, it becomes clear that the British have advanced well

beyond the German trenches and everywhere is deserted. The war is over.
They bury Jack Firebrace and Joseph Levi together. The next day, Levi and
Stephen exchange gifts and promise to write to each other, before Stephen
goes back to the British trenches to find his regiment. Despite his complete
mental and physical exhaustion, Stephen feels more alive than ever.

Main Points of Interest in Part Six

1. LEAVE WITH JEANNE
- Jeanne reveals that she loves Stephen.
- In his moment of sadness, it is clear that Stephen is still mourning over the loss of Isabelle.
- There are times when it seems there is some hope of Stephen and Jeanne being able to share a future together.

2. TRAPPED UNDERGROUND
- When the tunnel collapses, Stephen could choose to save himself, but instead decides to remain with Jack Firebrace.
- Jack is badly wounded, but Stephen remains optimistic about the chances of rescue.
- In his most lucid moments, Jack has clearly had enough of living and looks forward to death.
- Stephen never really gives up hope of being saved.

3. RESCUE
- Throughout the rescue attempt, Stephen believes that it is British tunnellers who are coming to save him.
- Levi's reaction to the loss of his brother shows him to be an honourable and deeply religious man.
- By the time Stephen is rescued, the war is over.

PART SEVEN - ENGLAND 1979

Elizabeth decides that the time has come to tell her mother of her pregnancy, even though she is unsure how Françoise will react. In the meantime, she has finished reading Stephen's translated notebooks. She reads of Stephen and Jack's entrapment underground, of Jack's love for his son, and Stephen's promise that he would bear children on Jack's behalf. Stephen's language towards Jeanne, is gentle, but not passionate. Elizabeth is confused by the dates in the notebook. She knows Jeanne's date of birth and marriage, but cannot reconcile this with her mother's age and her own date of birth.

Elizabeth and Françoise go out to dinner and eventually, Elizabeth plucks up the courage to tell her mother about her pregnancy. Françoise's reaction comes as a surprise - she is calm and accepting, even pleased. She reveals that she can hardly have any qualms about Elizabeth being unmarried, since her own parents were not married at the time of her birth. Elizabeth is confused by this, so Françoise explains that Elizabeth's grandmother, Jeanne, was not her natural mother: she is the daughter of Stephen and Isabelle. She was sent to live with Jeanne and Stephen in 1919, following Isabelle's death in the influenza epidemic. Françoise reveals that after the war she, Jeanne and Stephen had settled in Norfolk. Stephen, deeply traumatised by his wartime experiences, had remained silent for two years, but eventually began to speak again. She remembers that he spoiled her. He died at the age of 48, his health always having been poor. Jeanne, she recalls, loved him deeply and nursed him to the end of his life. She regrets that Stephen did not live to see Elizabeth. She believes that by doing so he would, somehow have been able to reconcile his feelings about his life and to see its purpose fulfilled.

In the few days before her baby is due to be born, Elizabeth and Robert rent a little cottage in the countryside. On their second night there, Elizabeth goes into labour. Robert telephones for the doctor, but she is unavailable, although her husband promises to send her to them as soon as possible. Robert must now take charge and, between him and Elizabeth, they manage to deliver the baby boy. The doctor arrives and Robert is dismissed to the garden. He wanders through a bed of conkers, filled with unexpected joy at the birth of his son, John, named in honour of Stephen's promise to Jack.

Main Points of Interest in Part Seven

1. FILLING IN THE GAPS

- It is confirmed by Françoise that she is Stephen and Isabelle's daughter.
- Françoise was raised by Jeanne and Stephen, who married shortly after the end of the war.
- Stephen's experiences in the war, left him so deeply affected that he did not speak for two years.
- The war took its toll on Stephen's health and he died at the age of 48, nursed to the end by Jeanne.

2. ELIZABETH'S BABY IS BORN

- Elizabeth gives birth to a baby boy, named John.
- Robert's reaction to the birth surprises even himself. Not only does he keep a clear head during the birth itself, but he is remarkably overcome by emotion and affection both for Elizabeth and John.

CHARACTER ANALYSIS

The creation of plausible characters is essential to the plot of any novel. The understanding of these characters is equally essential to the reader's appreciation of an individual piece of literature. In this chapter of the guide, I have taken each of the main characters in turn and given an analysis of their character traits. These analyses also contain some critical opinion of the portrayal of each character, which is based entirely on the viewpoint of the author of this guide.

1. STEPHEN WRAYSFORD

Stephen Wraysford is the common thread, who links all seven parts of this novel together. His complex character reveals him to be a survivor, a loner, a man desperately seeking a purpose to his life and longing to be something individual - or unique - rather than just another person. As the novel develops, the various experiences he undergoes shape his character further.

Stephen's childhood was harsh: he never met his father and his mother, having little time for him, left him in the care of his errant grandfather. Upon his grandfather's imprisonment, Stephen was placed in an institution, where, he believes, he lost his individuality and his sense of identity. The reader is given the impression that he has been trying to regain it ever since. Even when his grandfather was released from prison, his life did not improve and after becoming involved in a fight, he was sent back to the institution.

This was a place he grew to hate and he has no happy memories of his time there. It was while he was at the institution that he became more aware of his lifelong fear of birds. He touched a dead crow, in order to prove that he was not frightened of the birds, and this action has haunted him for the rest of his life. He had always hated birds, believing them to be savage creatures.

At this stage, a man named Vaughan offered to become his guardian. Stephen hoped that this would signify the beginning of a loving relationship, but Vaughan's interests were more academic than affectionate. Stephen was given a good education and Vaughan was also able to secure him a job, but he never treated the boy as his son. As a result of this, Stephen does not expect affection to be given to him, and finds it difficult to express his own feelings towards others.

Stephen's relationship with Isabelle is his first experience of love. He knows that his initial instinct towards her was sexual and predatory: he was determined that she would be his and the only doubt in his mind was how to go about achieving this. However, once he has accomplished his desire, he realises that his feelings towards her are very different to anything which he has ever experienced. He worships her unreservedly. His is a blind and overwhelming love which will admit of no weakness or imperfection on the part of his lover.

Stephen and Isabelle have such a passionate and intense affair, that one senses that it cannot possibly continue: it is too powerful and must eventually consume them. Through Isabelle, Stephen discovers that he is capable of caring deeply for others, and of inspiring their affection for him. His love and desire for Isabelle have, essentially, breathed life into him, to the extent that he is prepared to give up everything to continue his affair with her. She has become his reason for living.

Almost as soon as they leave Amiens, it becomes clear that their passion is not enough to provide them with a lasting relationship. Stephen, we are told, is 'lonely'. Living together is different from snatching odd moments of intimacy and he finds sharing a bed with Isabelle sometimes makes him 'uneasy'. He also becomes aware that Isabelle has changed towards him, but he knows that he has changed too and does not question this. He believes that this has come about simply due to the passage of time: that their relationship has changed and that the initial excitement has been replaced by a deep, mutual and lasting affection.

Isabelle's unexpected departure proves all of this to be wrong and triggers another change in Stephen's personality. He becomes withdrawn and isolated. The chasm created by her removal from his world is like an open wound that will not heal. He continues to live, of course, but in a world which he regards as second-best. He initially remains in their house in St Rémy, in the hope that she may reconsider her decision and return to him. Eventually, however, he realises that this will not happen, but even once he has accepted her departure, he cannot do so with any sense of healing or recovery. Instead he becomes numb to everything which surrounds him. When we meet Stephen again in the war, he is thought of as someone 'strange', or even 'mad' by his fellow soldiers. He claims that he never thinks of Isabelle, but this is not true and on the eve of the Battle of the Somme, it is to Isabelle that he writes a letter which he believes may be his last.

When they meet again in 1917, his continued love and desire for her are apparent. He is desperate to find out whether she still loves him, but is dealt another blow by the discovery that she now loves another man - a German. Outwardly he seems to accept this information with remarkable generosity of spirit, but in fact he retreats even further into himself. It is Jeanne who enables Stephen to perform the vital task of allowing himself to grieve.

The coming of war signifies further alterations to Stephen's character. While not feeling particularly patriotic, he returns to England to enlist. His desire to fight, and therefore release some of his repressed anger, becomes the fuel for his conviction that he must do his duty. As the war progresses, and Stephen witnesses more slaughter, he buries his emotions. He is uncomfortable with the men in his platoon - unsure what to say to them and how to respond to their fears and questions. He feels that they don't respect him, but can see that other officers around him are able to inspire such feelings in *their* men. It would seem, however, that his insecurity may have been unfounded as Brennan remembers Stephen as having a curious character, yet also recalls that he offered compassion to a dying man.

His feelings towards the war are complex. He naturally desires an end to the killing, but more than this, he wants to *understand* the war itself. He is awe-struck by man's capacity to suffer, and keep suffering, until told by some higher authority that they are allowed to stop. He believes that there must be some greater meaning to all the death and destruction surrounding him, and he wants to survive long enough to discover what that meaning is. He often seems unafraid at the prospect of his own death, yet if he is to die, he at least wants to understand *why*.

Gradually, his extreme mental and physical fatigue becomes overpowering. The war, death, imminent danger, suffering and grief have completely eroded his soul. He no longer feels anything. He has shut away his emotions and created a world of his own in which, as the war progresses, even he can no longer exist. At this stage, his saviour is Jeanne, who obviously cares very deeply for Stephen, and shows a great deal of understanding for the torture he has suffered. He also provides some salvation for himself. While on leave in Norfolk, he discovers that his life *does* have more meaning than the blood-soaked fields of Flanders. It is as though he is witnessing the beauty of the earth for the first time and he feels at one with nature. This gives his existence more of a purpose, which it had been lacking until this point.

The death of his friend, Weir, causes Stephen to once again re-evaluate his perception of the war. He envies the men who are taking part in the battle and his desire for revenge, against the men who have killed his friend, builds inside him. He feels profoundly lonely: he misses Weir's innocence and feels guilty that their final exchange came in a moment of anger. His life ceases to be a life and becomes an existence - merely a state of being.

During Stephen's entrapment underground with Jack Firebrace, he undergoes a multitude of emotions. He is aware that, in saving Jack, he has potentially forfeited his own life - he had the opportunity to escape, but saved Jack instead. He is prepared to die, yet when faced with the opportunity to live, he grasps it enthusiastically, and will not let go. He wants Jack to survive too. He knows that he owes his life to Jack and, having carried him on his back up and down the tunnels, and worked for days to bring about their release, he is disappointed that Jack succumbs so willingly, and gratefully, to death.

Stephen's meeting with his rescuer, Levi, marks a turning point. His initial euphoria at being saved, is tempered with disappointment that his saviour is, in fact, his enemy. However, he cannot fight this man, and instead, seeks the comfort of a fellow human being. Both of these men have suffered greatly and, regardless of what is to follow, neither can bring himself to take another life - turning instead to friendship. Stephen's experiences in the war obviously cause him great mental anguish and we learn, through his granddaughter's investigations, that he remained mute for two years after the fighting had ended. It would seem that his need to understand was greater than his need to communicate.

Stephen Wraysford's character undergoes many changes during the course of the novel, all of which are caused by external influences: childhood deprivation; passionate, yet unfulfilled love; constant fear of death; visions of suffering and destruction. These events have a catastrophic effect on Stephen, yet he survives.

CRITICAL OPINION OF THE PORTRAYAL OF STEPHEN WRAYSFORD

In Stephen Wraysford, Sebastian Faulks has created an enigma. He is open, yet private; 'strange' yet straightforward; loving yet detached; aloof yet 'craving' friendship. This is very confusing and leads the reader to keep asking the question: 'Why?' Why does Stephen accept promotion through the ranks when this seems out of character? Why does he hate Germans? Why does Stephen dabble in the occult? Many of the answers lie not in the character himself, but in the author's need to link various aspects of the plot, or to explain or introduce certain elements of the First World War. So, for example, Stephen's ability to see into the future crops up from time to time, such as in the cathedral at Amiens, when he foresees 'a terrible piling up of the dead'. But, does he, or does he not have second sight? Does he 'fix' the cards, when he tells Weir's fortune? Or is this all just a means of linking the war scenes back to the first part of the novel and giving Stephen's character a 'mysterious' air? In any case, would someone as cynical as Stephen Wraysford, believe in the occult in the first place? Equally, Stephen's hatred of Germans, which rises far above any of his comrades' feelings towards the enemy, is given no logical explanation. However, this is necessary to the plot, as he must later learn to accept that Isabelle has chosen a life of exile with a

German soldier, and that he will eventually owe his life to a German rescuer. This helps Sebastian Faulks to introduce the theme of forgiveness and in order for that to work better, it is necessary that Stephen's character should hate Germans.

Part of the problem with Wraysford's character, leading one to ask these questions, is that it is not sufficiently well-drawn. There is too much veneer and not enough depth. As the central, pivotal character, the reader needs to be able to understand his actions and reactions, but often there is not enough explanation. We are told, on more than one occasion, that Stephen is 'strange', but we are not told in what way. We are told that he is terrified of birds, but the explanation given seems insufficient for such an extreme reaction. He is described as 'mad' but we do not know why or how.

At the beginning of the novel, he is introduced as twenty years old, quiet, shy, and with an air of mystery about him. With the exception of Isabelle, however, almost every other adult in Part One of the novel, is given a thoroughly disagreeable character, so Stephen's seems much more appealing and interesting. His affair with Isabelle begins hastily and is based purely on physical lust - which he is determined to see fulfilled. His feelings later develop into love, we are told, but he still seems deeply uncomfortable in her presence. There is no adequate explanation for his discomfort or for his 'loneliness'. He does not seem to share Isabelle's sense of guilt or shame, so why are most of his emotions at this time so negative?

Throughout their affair, Stephen has demonstrated an inner strength, convincing Isabelle that their feelings for one another are sufficient grounds for their actions. Despite this, one senses that he has always realised that their affair could not last. So why does Isabelle's departure come as such a shock and cause such a reaction? One could argue that he initially behaves quite reasonably, given the depth of his affections, but to continue to feel so cold and distant and to exclude all other sexual relationships from his life, for seven years, seems a little excessive, especially given the supposed strength of his character. The purpose behind this reaction, however, could be to demonstrate the true strength of Jeanne's character and her relationship with Stephen. Their connection develops more slowly and is not based on sex, but on friendship and support. They talk more and gradually Jeanne falls in love with Stephen. He never openly declares his love for her, but we know it is there. These episodes show that love, not passion, hatred, lust or fear, is the emotion that really matters.

When we meet Stephen again, in 1916, the overriding impression given is that he is a 'strange', German-hating officer with little respect of or for his men. However, given his experiences and circumstances, his actions are not really that 'strange', forcing many of the characters to have to point out this trait, somewhat clumsily in order to get the point across. Sergeant Adams, Gray, Weir and Brennan, at various times, all tell us that Stephen is 'strange' or 'mad' and yet his actions do not seem to really bear this out. Yes, he dabbles in the occult - but he does not take it seriously; yes, he is aloof from his men, but that was not uncommon, especially among officers who had been promoted through the ranks. His desire to understand the war, to make sense of the killing, rather than just to see it all end with no explanation, is not described well enough to enable us to see this element of his character as particularly 'strange'. Why shouldn't he want to know why so many men have died? All of this, therefore, seems to be an attempt to make his character seem still more mysterious: to give him an air of obscurity, without taking the time to explain it.

Stephen's fear of birds is important to the story in that it is a horror which must be overcome in order for Stephen's character to flourish, but also because it links to the title of the novel. When Stephen is underground with Weir, it would seem that he is more worried about carrying the canary than he is about being buried underground. However, we have already been told that he has a 'long horror' of confined spaces. That being the case, one wonders why he had asked to see the tunnels in the first place. These phobias, therefore, feel contrived.

Stephen's character flits between hope and despair with almost reckless abandon. One minute he is in the depths of depression and hopelessness; the next he is looking forward to a brighter and more optimistic future than he ever thought possible. While on leave in Norfolk, he seems to miraculously and inexplicably find an inner peace, while walking in the fields. This soon fades, without an explanation for its coming or its going. When he returns to France, he is more depressed than ever and finally breaks down.

Within a very short time, however, when forced to face his own death, he finds that he is not prepared to die and fights to survive, against all the odds. However, by this time Stephen has undergone so many changes of heart and mind, that the reader is almost tempted to question whether they really care what happens to him anymore.

2. ISABELLE AZAIRE

Like Stephen, Isabelle is the product of a difficult childhood, greatly affected by external events and the circumstances in which she finds herself.

The youngest of five sisters, Isabelle has never had high expectations of her life, assuming that she would remain with her parents and care for them in their old age. She feels that she has always inspired disappointment in others. She craved love and affection but her parents were indifferent to her, being too absorbed in their own lives to pay her much attention, except when it seemed likely that she might marry unwisely. Her romance with a young soldier, Jean Destournel, was quickly terminated by her father, who deemed the match unsuitable. Isabelle developed her own individuality - slightly aloof, refined, but with definite and distinctive ideas and tastes. This independent streak made her parents uncomfortable, so her father took the first opportunity to marry her to a suitable man. Throughout her life, Isabelle's only friend and confidante, has been her sister Jeanne.

Isabelle's marriage to René Azaire was arranged between her father and Azaire and Isabelle consented partly through her desire to escape from her parents, and also because of her pity for Azaire's children who had lost their own mother. Azaire's reasons for marrying Isabelle are more to do with appearance and reputation. She is poised and beautiful but also young enough to bear him more children. Isabelle submits to his sexual demands, but neither finds, nor expects love or passion in their relationship. Her failure to become pregnant reflects badly on Azaire, both publicly and privately. In public, he alludes to her headaches and paints a picture of her as troublesome and nervous, which provides an acceptable public excuse for him being unable to have sex with his wife. Privately, he finds that he has become physically incapable of making love, and resorts to violence as a means of arousal. Isabelle, however, does not blame him; she pities him. She is not happy, but accepts that this has been her choice in life. She becomes a victim of these choices, suppressing her own desires and emotions and submitting to a mundane existence, until the arrival of Stephen Wraysford.

The sexual and emotional tension between Isabelle and Stephen is obvious almost from their first meeting. Isabelle cannot look at him; she can barely talk to him and when he first approaches her, she rejects him, fearing the consequences of a liaison, and unsure of her own reactions. Guilt and propriety initially force her to keep her growing desires in check.

Ultimately, Isabelle relents, but what she had not anticipated was the huge outpouring of lust and emotion which Stephen would inspire in her. Despite her inexperience in many sexual matters, she finds that her enjoyment of it is instinctive. It is as though Stephen has given meaning to her life. She is unable to help herself, or control her feelings for him. Through him, she is able to really *feel* for the first time in her life - however the intensity of her desire for Stephen makes her uncomfortable.

Isabelle is also unsure of Stephen's feelings for her. Although he has expressed his love for her, she still appears to think that something is missing from their relationship and that too much importance has been placed on their physical desires. Their departure from the Boulevard du Cange is, essentially, at her instigation and yet almost immediately her feelings of guilt begin to engulf her. When their initial feelings of lust and passion have naturally subsided, rather than being left with a deeper emotion of love, Isabelle is only left with feelings of guilt.

The discovery of her pregnancy exacerbates her anxiety and she begins to blame herself for the actions she and Stephen have taken. She believes that any potential danger to her baby is her fault and that by leaving Stephen, she may be able to absolve herself. She is also unsure whether the type of love they share is strong enough to sustain them through the difficult times ahead. She still cares for Stephen, and probably always will, but her feelings for him have been overtaken by her strong passion for the baby she is carrying, so she seeks solace with the only person she knows she can trust - Jeanne.

By the time the First World War begins, Isabelle has returned to the Boulevard du Cange and resumed her life with René. This was not a willing decision on her part, but was borne of her deep unhappiness at having to live with her parents again and the need to provide a secure home for her child. The war has proved to be a salvation for Isabelle - it has removed Azaire from her life and given her the opportunity to start again. Her meeting with Max has provided her life with meaning once again and she feels more comfortable with him, despite his nationality. This relationship is completely different - gone is the ardent passion and intense desire. With Max she feels a more satisfying sense of sharing and companionship, amounting to a deeper love, which she knows will last longer than anything she shared with Stephen.

Her facial injury has not diminished her, but made her stronger and more determined to find happiness. Her decision to keep their daughter's existence a secret from Stephen is interesting. One could argue that she is putting her daughter's happiness first. Equally, however, one could say that this is the final, most cruel betrayal of Stephen. She knows that if she tells Stephen about their daughter, he will want to become a part of their lives. This will complicate her happy relationship with Max, so she keeps the little girl a secret. To deny Stephen this knowledge, when he already has so little, is intensely heartless.

The meeting between Stephen and Isabelle shows that he is still able to easily arouse her sexually, just by touching her. Her passion has not diminished, but this time she will not surrender herself: she has a child of her own now and believes that her own continued happiness and the security of her daughter are better ensured either alone or with Max, than they are with Stephen.

Ultimately, Isabelle forfeits everything to go to Max when he is injured. On leaving France she knows that she will never be able to return and will be, forever, an outcast. Unlike when she was outcast by her relationship with Stephen, she feels that this time the sacrifices are worth making.

CRITICAL OPINION OF THE PORTRAYAL OF ISABELLE AZAIRE

Isabelle Azaire's character is one which could be interpreted in one of two ways. Either she is a victim of her circumstances, used by men and manipulated into situations beyond her control; or she is a selfish creature, who puts her own feelings ahead of everyone else's. Her childhood and marriage would seem to point to the former: her father had dictated her marriage to Azaire and, once married, Azaire controls every aspect of her life. However, marriage has also suited Isabelle. It has allowed her to escape from her overbearing dictatorial father and she lives a comfortable life, financially secure, with more freedom than many of her contemporaries would have enjoyed. The one feature of her life which seems intolerable, is Azaire's brutal treatment of her. Even in this, she has to admit that he does not physically hurt her and that the torment is more humiliating than anything else. She acknowledges also that he shames himself more than her by his actions and that she feels pity rather than hatred for him.

Stephen's arrival opens Isabelle's eyes to the one aspect of her life which has, hitherto, been missing: passion. She succumbs to Stephen's advances relatively willingly; her desire for him clearly being stronger than her sense of decency. Having submitted, she becomes the stronger partner of the two: she begins to dictate the timing and frequency of their meetings; she demands that Stephen should not show his affection when in the presence of Azaire; she initiates their departure from the Boulevard du Cange. Although she believes that he 'makes her do things', everything that she does is of her own free will.

Isabelle's decision to leave Stephen is another demonstration of her strong determination. She becomes pregnant and cherishes her unborn child to the exclusion of all else, including Stephen. She seems to no longer wish him to be part of her life and does not tell him of the pregnancy, but leaves him with no idea of what has happened or why she has taken this course. Even to Azaire, who had treated her wish such harshness, she shows more sympathy than she does to Stephen. Her subsequent choice of leaving France to be with Max shows that, for him, she is prepared to sacrifice everything, while Stephen was, somehow, less worthy.

Overall, one has to wonder at Sebastian Faulks portrayal of this woman. She is at once harsh and selfish, but also appealing and captivating. The reader, even while acknowledging her self-interest, cannot fail to sympathise with her. This is quite a clever representation. Her repressed passionate nature makes the reader feel more compassionate with regard to her loveless marriage and one feels pleased that she has, at last, found love with Stephen. However, her subsequent treatment of him forces the reader to sympathise instead with Stephen, and to explain some of his subsequent actions. In addition, Isabelle's less generous characteristics are a foil to Jeanne's more sensitive and compassionate nature - and she, of course, is the woman with whom Stephen ultimately spends the remainder of his life.

Each character and their actions are placed into the novel for a purpose and Isabelle is no different. The romance between Isabelle and Stephen is supposed to demonstrate that passion and lust are not sufficient feelings to enable a lasting relationship. No matter how strong or overwhelming these sensations may be, once they have died down, if all that is left is guilt, then there is no hope. And that is precisely the atmosphere into which Faulks wishes Stephen to be placed: a life devoid of hope, love, caring or humanity; filled instead with war, death and hatred. From there, he can, with the help of true friends like Jeanne and Weir, rebuild himself and find something positive from the depths of despair.

3. JACK FIREBRACE

Jack is one of the tunnellers, whose job is to dig out under No Man's Land. The purpose of this is two-fold: firstly to lay charges under the German trenches, which, when exploded cause massive damage and general confusion, allowing the attacking force an element of surprise. The second reason for tunnelling is to listen to enemy activity. Jack's background has always been as a miner. In London, he worked on the digging of the London Underground. His family are not well off; in fact when war broke out, Jack was unemployed and, believing that the war would soon be over, he enlisted. At thirty-eight, he is older than many of his colleagues, and seems to have earned their respect. He is married, with an eight year old son, named John, whom he idolises.

Jack must contemplate his own mortality quite early in the story. Having fallen asleep while on sentry duty, he is caught by Weir and Wraysford and faces a court martial which may result in possible execution by firing squad. Alone with his thoughts, he realises that, despite witnessing an obscene amount of death and destruction, he is unprepared for the end of his own life. It is not that he believes himself to be more deserving of preservation than anyone else, but just that he longs to be allowed to live and see his wife and son again. He is deeply worried about his son's illness and misses him terribly. Neither Weir nor Wraysford is willing or able to go through with the court martial, so Jack is spared. However, his request for leave to go and see his sick son is refused as he cannot be spared.

Despite being surrounded by death every day, and, in fact, becoming immune to it, Jack cannot face the death of his own son. He postpones reading letters from his wife, for fear that they will contain the long-dreaded news. When John dies, Jack is completely devastated. Up to this point he had not really appreciated just how much John meant to him and how empty life will be without him. These thoughts do not immediately come to him, however and his initial emotions centre around the fact that he and his wife should remember their son and be grateful to God for his presence in their lives

Throughout all of this heartbreak Jack's faith in God remains intact. His beliefs, however, are shaken on 1st July 1916, when, standing behind the lines in an elevated position, he looks down on the carnage of the battlefield. Unable to accept this level of destruction, Jack becomes aware that his trust in God has died. He cannot believe that his God would allow the wholesale destruction of so many lives. The Somme has destroyed something within him, which even the death of his own son had been unable to shake.

As the war progresses, Jack witnesses his fair share of death. Most of his friends are killed and gradually his own determination to survive is waning. When Jack is finally faced with his own death, he accepts it gladly, feeling that he has nothing left to give and no desire to live in the world this war has created. He senses that the existence that they all had before the war, will have been destroyed and that nothing will ever be the same. Even his desire to see his wife again has diminished. He knows that he will never be able to share his experiences with her, and that in death he will be with people who understand what he has become, far better than the living ever could.

CRITICAL OPINION OF THE PORTRAYAL OF JACK FIREBRACE

Jack's role in the novel is partially to demonstrate how much the human soul can tolerate. His faith survives the death of his son, but is shattered by the carnage of the Somme. He shows us that men were prepared to push themselves to the very limits, but would then reach a point where they could go no further. He also represents the ordinary working-class man, for whom the war was not so much a duty as a necessity. With little work available at home and money being in short supply, his reason for enlisting had essentially been financial. Despite this, he remains one of the most hard-working and diligent of the soldiers in the novel. Jack is basically everything that all the others aspire to. He is able, willing, popular and respected, both among his comrades and the officers. And yet, at the very end of the novel - at the very end of the war - he is killed. The purpose of this is to demonstrate not only the pointless nature of the war, in that the best men die, but also to show how much Stephen - who seems to have so much less to live for - has overcome in order to survive.

In addition, Jack's role is to give Stephen hope. When Jack begins to despair, it is Stephen who urges him on. When Jack explains that he and his wife will not be able to have any more children, Stephen says he will have them on Jack's behalf. Eventually, of course, Stephen does not have any more children, but he already has one: Françoise. Elizabeth is then able to complete the circle, by naming her son after Jack's dead boy. This provides a complete resolution to the plot. Elizabeth, having learnt of the hardships and suffering of the war, feels indebted to that generation and, when the opportunity arises, fulfils her grandfather's promise.

Jack's sense of disconnection with the world and his dread of returning to it after the war, fuel his desire to embrace death. This is a common trait amongst literature of the First World War, where authors are keen to demonstrate how the experiences of the trenches would forever change the participants.

Jack represents some of the unsung heroes of the war. Not everybody went charging 'over the top' but all made a contribution and Jack's role is to show that, frequently, these men were just as brave and deserving as the more acclaimed heroes. Sebastian Faulks clearly wanted to retell their story and Jack's character provides him with the necessary vehicle and links many parts of the story together.

4. MICHAEL WEIR

Captain Michael Weir is a member of the Royal Engineers, who has been assigned to command a company of tunnellers. He is thirty-two years old, and during the course of the novel, becomes Stephen's best friend. These two men are often to be found together, much to the chagrin of Stephen's senior officers, who believe that the tunnellers and the infantry should not mix.

Weir comes from a respectable and quiet background, living with his parents in Leamington Spa. He has had little experience of life and none whatsoever of women. In order to escape this stifling existence, Weir joined the Royal Engineers in 1912 finding that, although he still had no particular friends, the surroundings and company were, at least favourable to the life he had known before. In addition, this enforced separation from women has enabled him to hide his sexual inexperience - he has become just like all the other men who have to endure life without the comfort of a woman.

As a professional soldier, Weir did not initially look upon the outbreak of war with any degree of fear. In fact, according to Stephen, Weir had 'liked the war' at the beginning. As the conflict has progressed, however, Weir has gained a reputation as an unconventional officer, whose enthusiasm has gradually been worn down by the war and his experiences. He does not relish his underground existence, often finding excuses to remain above ground, and has become more and more dependent on whisky and Stephen. When Weir believes that Stephen is dead, he can see little point in continuing to live himself. He decides that he will 'court' death, since without Stephen, he cannot see much point in living anymore.

Like many of the men, he comes to regard Stephen as something of a good-luck charm and frequently asks him to tell his fortune. This makes their angry parting very difficult for Weir who feels he has been betrayed. Stephen has always envied Weir's innocence and looks upon it as a trait which he lost long ago.

During his leave, Weir becomes angry about the complacency of those at home. This, however, could be said to reflect not only his general state of depression, but also his difficult relationship with his parents. His father is unwilling to listen to Weir's explanations of the war, believing that he has all the information he needs from the newspaper reports. Weir feels that he no longer belongs at home and when he returns to the front, his hatred for those at home is obvious and extreme.

CRITICAL OPINION OF THE PORTRAYAL OF MICHAEL WEIR

The purpose of Weir's character in the novel is to provide Stephen's first real taste of friendship. In addition, for probably the first time in his life, Weir represents someone to whom Stephen can be of use and for whom he eventually starts to feel responsible. Weir is an innocent, while the younger Wraysford, is much more worldly-wise and Stephen respects Weir's innocent nature as representing something which he lost many many years ago - before the war even started. As such Weir represents the antithesis of Stephen's character. This representation would, however, work better if, like Stephen, there could be a more thorough explanation of Weir's supposed 'strangeness'. The descriptions of him differ, but he invariably seems to be more eccentric than strange.

Another role for Weir's character is to show the reader the arrogance of the home front. His spell of leave tells us how much more 'friendly' he finds life in the trenches and tunnels of Western Front, compared to his stifling existence at home. His parents barely acknowledge his presence, seeming more concerned with their own sacrifices in the war and are completely disinterested in hearing anything about his experiences. Sebastian Faulks has chosen to represent the home front in this way and Weir provides a useful vehicle. His reactions are heartfelt and natural, forcing the reader to take his response seriously and feel incredulous at his parent's heartlessness - probably the very reaction which Faulks was hoping to inspire. One should remember, however, that Weir's character is not necessarily portrayed as the most stable of those represented in the novel, in the first place.

Weir's death, needless as it is, also provides a turning point for Stephen in that it allows him to acknowledge his love and dependence on his dead friend - something which he would have found more difficult to do while Weir was still alive. Stephen mourns for him in a more emotional way than he had done when Isabelle had abandoned him. At that time, he had quietly gone on as before, outwardly appearing the same and only allowing himself to grieve in the privacy of his own home. Upon Weir's death, however, Stephen takes to his bed and is only roused by the ministrations of Colonel Gray. In this way, Sebastian Faulks is telling his readers that the relationships formed in the trenches could be more significant than those with parents or lovers.

5. JEANNE FOURMENTIER

Jeanne, as Françoise points out, is the 'heroine of the the whole story'. She has always protected Isabelle and, in turn, looks after Stephen too. She is tolerant, generous and does not judge others. Her patience is unlimited and she cares very deeply for both her sister and Stephen. Hers is a quiet heroism, in that, without her, neither of the two main characters would be able to achieve their own individual happiness, yet her part is unobtrusive.

Her initial reaction to Stephen's appearance in Amiens during the war is to distrust his motives. She, of course, knows that Isabelle is relatively happy and settled with her daughter, and does not wish Stephen to complicate matters for her sister. Later, when she writes to Stephen, we learn that without her, he would be alone in the world and, although he is unsure how he should respond to her, he welcomes her friendship. Jeanne is significantly older than Stephen and her wisdom helps him to understand his position, both in Isabelle's life and in the war.

The nature of the relationship between Jeanne and Stephen is very different to the passionate affair which he had shared with Isabelle. There is no sexual contact between Jeanne and Stephen and even when Jeanne contemplates this, it is only as a means of raising Stephen's spirits. However, she appreciates that this would only complicate matters between them and the sex would be forced, rather than impulsive, and would therefore prove ultimately less than satisfying, both mentally and physically. Although Jeanne may be more quiet and dispassionate than her sister, she seems to want her relationship with Stephen to be as important to him as it is to her.

Jeanne provides Stephen with the one thing which he lacks in his friendships at the front: someone in whom he can confide. Weir always turns to Stephen for comfort and encouragement, but Stephen has no-one to perform this task for him - except Jeanne. When he begins to doubt his own ability to continue to fight, she inspires him to return to the front and to do his duty. Her declaration of love is understated and heartfelt - probably because she has nothing to gain by this announcement and is fully aware that Stephen's feelings towards her sister are still undiminished. She, however, risks everything to secure his happiness and security. She realises that some might believe there to be some impropriety in her forming an attachment to her sister's former lover, but Jeanne consoles herself with the knowledge that the man with whom she is in love is a very different person to the man who knew and loved Isabelle.

CRITICAL OPINION OF THE PORTRAYAL OF JEANNE FOURMENTIER

If one believes that Isabelle is really rather a selfish creature, then Jeanne is surely the opposite. Her character provides stability in Isabelle's early life and it is to Jeanne that Isabelle always turns when she finds herself in difficulty. The portrayal of Jeanne as such a patient and understanding character, always there to answer Isabelle's requirements, could lead one to dismiss her as a compliant, minor character, whose role is somewhat trivial. This is to do her an injustice. She is more than capable of looking after herself and demonstrates this when she chooses to remain away from her parents, not even telling them of her presence in Rouen. She knows that they would wish to dominate her life again, but she wishes to seek a new life for herself with Stephen.

Her understanding and acceptance of Stephen's obsession with Isabelle could be seen as a form of desperation on her part. One could argue that she is no longer young and wishes to finally escape from her parents so she seems happy to settle for her sister's discarded lover, at a time when single men of marriageable age are becoming a rarity. To accept this theory, however, belies Jeanne's own wisdom. She knows that Isabelle and Stephen shared a passionate relationship - they have produced a daughter to prove it. She also knows how destructive their affair has been, both to themselves and to almost everyone around them. She wants, instead, to care for Stephen, acknowledging that the war has left him a broken man. She does not offer this out of gratitude or desperation, but out of love.

In addition, her acceptance of his relationship with Isabelle allows him to grieve for her. When he breaks down in Jeanne's arms, sobbing Isabelle's name, the reader could feel that she might be more inclined to feel offended and possibly reject him. However, her character is not jealous of this earlier affair and her intelligence allows her to appreciate that he needs to get Isabelle completely out of his system before she and Stephen can possibly move on and form a relationship of their own. This portrayal enables the reader to sympathise even more with Jeanne, but also to acknowledge that this is the first time that Stephen has found himself in a position to express his feelings and that it is Jeanne who has made this possible.

Jeanne's love for her niece, Françoise, is also made clear. In the modern sections of the novel, we learn that, not only did she care deeply for Stephen and nurse him until his death, but she also provided Françoise with a stable and happy childhood. Sebastian Faulks has created here a selfless and loving character, showing us the best side of humanity and assuring us that hope is never lost entirely.

6. ELIZABETH BENSON

Elizabeth Benson is the main character in the modern section of the book and, we discover, is Stephen and Isabelle's grand-daughter. She is an independent woman, with an artistic streak, possibly inherited from Stephen. She is unmarried but has a relationship with a married man named Robert, who will not divorce his wife because they have a daughter whom he wishes to protect. Elizabeth is, although she will not always acknowledge it, keen to have a baby and this desire builds as her story progresses.

Elizabeth develops an obsession with discovering her family background. She wants to know where she came from, feeling that if she does have a child, she can pass on the information she has discovered, but even if she remains childless, she wants to understand her past, and therefore, herself. Finding out about Stephen takes her on a journey, both physically and emotionally as she discovers more about his life and involvement in the First World War. She had previously had no idea what the First World War had involved and is shocked to discover the number of men who died. In meeting with Brennan, she also finds out that for those who survived, life could become simply a confused mass of memories.

She is overjoyed when she becomes pregnant and her independence does not allow her to be swayed into any safe options: she will keep her baby, even if she has to raise it alone. Her own mother had to raise Elizabeth almost single-handed, since her husband left when Elizabeth was a baby, returning only when it suited him. This upbringing would have given Elizabeth a viewpoint that women can and should be capable of doing whatever they want with their own lives. Her pregnancy also heightens her desire to understand her background, and complete the circle.

CRITICAL OPINION OF THE PORTRAYAL OF ELIZABETH BENSON

Elizabeth Benson is probably the most contrived character, in the most contrived sections of the novel. Her sole purpose within the story is to retell the missing parts of Stephen's life and to link these to a modern perception of the First World War. Her affair with Robert mirrors the snatched, illicit relationship between Isabelle and Stephen in Part One; her pregnancy, much longed-for, but awkward when it eventually happens, also reflects the situation in which Isabelle had found herself. Elizabeth's visit to the memorial at Thiepval, commemorating the missing of the Somme, is rather coincidental, given that Stephen's Battalion had been in action there.

We are told that she reads about the First World War and is 'troubled', but not how or why. Her 'mild curiosity' rapidly and for no apparent reason, becomes a 'set determination' to find out more about her grandfather. Her need to 'understand more about herself' seems incongruous, but imitates Stephen's lust for knowledge about the war while he had been fighting in it. However, Elizabeth is a young, independent, single woman, who runs her own business, travels, has a married lover, and lives a pleasant life. Given all of that it seems hard to believe that she does not 'understand' herself.

Several parts of Elizabeth's character seem to have been forced into the story. Her mother, Françoise, for example, fondly remembers Stephen's presence in her life and yet when Elizabeth asks her about him, both women seem embarrassed. For someone who is so naturally inquisitive and desirous of knowledge as Elizabeth is meant to be, this hesitancy on the part of both women seems simply to be a way of drawing out the plot to enable her to more gradually discover her grandfather's character and story.

THEMES AND COMPARISONS

In this section I have provided analysis of some of the main themes of the novel *Birdsong*, looking at how Sebastian Faulks has portrayed them and their impact on the reader's interpretation of the novel. In addition, I have also given some detailed comparisons with how other authors and occasionally poets, have dealt with similar topics.

1. MALE RELATIONSHIPS

The portrayal of relationships between men in the literature of the First World War depends greatly in the time during which the piece was written. Many of the authors writing in this genre in the second half of the twentieth century, especially in the last 15-20 years, have been able to do much more than hint at the nature of these relationships and have portrayed some of them as openly and graphically homosexual. Those who were writing just after the end of the First World War, however, were not even able to suggest homosexuality, but referred instead to hero-worship and close, but chaste, male friendships.

In *Birdsong*, Sebastian Faulks has portrayed his main character, Stephen Wraysford, especially during the war scenes, as unapproachable and difficult. He does, however, have a particular friend: Michael Weir. Despite certain similarities in their characters, theirs is a peculiar friendship, in that it is based on the needs of one party. Weir's nerves have got the better of him and he depends on alcohol and Stephen's strength of character to keep going. It is only after Weir's death that Stephen can even begin to understand the value of this friendship to himself and regrets his shabby treatment of Weir at their last meeting. It could be argued that this friendship had begun as a form of hero-worship, in that Weir had looked up to Stephen, making their relationship very one-sided. However, it must also be remembered that Stephen's character is very cold, so his need for a particular friend is diminished, while Weir seems desperate for someone to console him.

The portrayal of this level and type of relationship is fairly common in First World War novels and plays. The friendship between Stanhope and Osborne in R. C. Sherriff's *Journey's End* is similar in many ways to the one in *Birdsong*. Stanhope has undergone so much trauma during his time at the front, that he can no longer function without alcohol and the help of his dearest companion, Osborne. In this respect the characters of Stanhope and Weir are very similar. Both men have seen too much of the war and wish only for it to end. Osborne, on the other hand, is a strong, former schoolmaster, with great warmth and kindness, who regards the other members of the company as his family. He is very protective of Stanhope and defends his reputation against anyone who doubts his ability to command the company. In this instance, it is Osborne who dies and Stanhope who is left to face the future alone. However, that future is very short-lived, as the company is about to go into battle.

There is a second relationship in *Journey's End*, which also bears comparison with the portrayal of the friendship between Wraysford and Weir. Stanhope's company is joined in the trenches by one of his former schoolfriends, Raleigh, who had worshipped the popular, slightly older Stanhope throughout their time at school. This previous relationship places Stanhope in an awkward position as his character has changed so much during the war, that he knows Raleigh will find it difficult to accept him as the same person. To avoid facing this situation, Stanhope keeps his distance from Raleigh. This relationship is used to portray the effects of war on an individual and how much people can change when placed in such circumstances.

Both Stanhope and Wraysford are forced to accept their situations and, in both cases, are made stronger by their losses. In Stanhope's case, he manages to come to the aid of his old school friend, Raleigh, comforting him as he lies dying. Stephen Wraysford, on the other hand, has longer to come to terms with Weir's death and it does seem to transform him, making him more accepting and friendly towards the other men. When he is buried underground with Jack Firebrace, he puts the well-being of the other man first, risking his own life in the process. This is not an action which the reader could easily associate with Stephen's character, prior to Weir's death. In both of these texts, while these relationships do not exactly come under the heading of 'hero-worship', they are definitely based on the needs of one party, for the company of the other.

Other types of male friendship are also explored in the literature of this period. Simple comradeship is probably the most common form of relationship formed in the trenches and this can be seen in most novels and plays of, or about, the First World War. In *Birdsong*, one could look at the friendships between Jack Firebrace and his fellow tunnellers, especially Arthur Shaw. We are told that Jack's first two friends had been killed early in the war and that he had been reluctant to form any new friendships. Before long, however, he comes to think of Arthur Shaw as the 'only person in the world'. Their relationship is portrayed with the same level of comfort and affection as Jack's marriage - in a purely non-sexual way. They sleep alongside one another, curled up comfortably; they share all their troubles. Shaw's death brings about a change in Jack, in that despite his efforts to appear happy-go-lucky, he is numb. He remembers Shaw as someone whom he loved 'more than my heart would bear', in which he is comparing this with his love for John, his only son.

This type of close friendship is commonly portrayed in many of the memoirs and poems written by those who participated in the First World War. Edmund Blunden's *Undertones of War*, first published in 1928, recounts with great fondness, his remembrance of his war-time friendships. Many of these were between himself and his fellow officers, such as Swain - 'a man whose warmth of heart often cheers me... a plain, brave, affectionate man.' At other times, however, he speaks with great respect and warmth of the men under his command. Blunden had been in training at Shoreham and had been in command of a squad of men who had already seen action in the trenches and were awaiting their orders to return. He describes in his memoirs their sense of contentment, peace and comradeship, together with their willingness to protect him, a novice, from what they knew would lie ahead. In his poem *1916 Seen From 1921*, Blunden describes himself as 'Dead as the men I loved', and speaks of his attempts to find such friendships after the war, but finding 'none'. It is clear from both his prose and poetry, that Blunden was, like many who had experienced the war, haunted by his losses and by the friends who had lived with him through those horrors, which no non-combatant could ever really understand.

Male relationships are occasionally portrayed in a more intense manner. This does not necessarily mean that these are physical, homosexual relationships, although that is not always ruled out. One such example is the portrayal of the friendship between Siegfried Sassoon and Wilfred Owen in Pat Barker's *Regeneration*. Here, we can see many of the elements described earlier: hero-worship, mutual respect and close male bonding, based on shared experiences. However, there are also stark differences. The first of these is that this relationship has its basis in fact. Sassoon and Owen did, indeed, meet at and form a close alliance. In addition, this was not a friendship which was formed in the trenches, but in the confines of Craiglockhart Military Hospital, where both men, for different reasons, were undergoing treatment. Their friendship was based, initially at least, on Wilfred Owen's hero-worship of Sassoon, the poet. It was only as their friendship blossomed, that Sassoon began to develop a respect for Owen's poetry. He introduced the younger man to some of his many literary friends and helped to improve Owen's faltering self-confidence. In reality, it is a matter of debate as to whether these two men had a physical relationship, but in the novel it is deemed that most of the attraction is on Owen's side. Upon his departure, we are told, Owen finds the loss of Sassoon's company overwhelming and later, when he has returned to training, he writes 'effusive' letters to his friend, which cause Sassoon to worry that Owen may have perceived something more in their relationship than he had intended. This may, however, have more to do with Sassoon's own confusion as to his feelings for his fellow officers and towards men in general.

In reality, this clearly was a very deep and intense friendship, whether physical or not, and Sassoon, in his memoir *Siegfried's Journey*, describes his feelings of 'deprivation' following Owen's death. He wrote this memoir in 1945, 27 years after the end of the war and yet he reveals that 'even now it has needed an effort of will to describe our friendship.'

Strong, emotional (and potentially physical) attachments, such as this, are also depicted in the novels of the First World War, such as Susan Hill's *Strange Meeting*. Here, John Hilliard and David Barton meet in France for the first time and, although Hilliard, like Stephen Wraysford, is reluctant to form any friendships whatsoever, he and Barton soon become extremely close, with Hilliard coming to depend greatly on the younger officer's optimism, kindness and generosity. They become almost inseparable and, when they are apart, Hilliard finds himself in a blind panic as to what he would do if anything were to happen to Barton. They eventually declare their love for one another, in a surprisingly easy and open manner, given Hilliard's emotional reticence. Susan Hill has stated in her 'Afterword', that she did not necessarily 'intend the conclusion to be drawn that Barton and Hilliard had a physical relationship' and this aspect, it must be said, is completely irrelevant in the context of the story. Upon reading this novel, one is not concerned with the physical particulars of their lives, but with their emotional bond which Barton sums up with the words: 'Things don't happen like this often in a lifetime.'

2. PORTRAYAL OF LOVE AND SEX

Unlike many other First World War novels, Sebastian Faulks makes no mention of homosexual relationships, although there is a brief moment of homo-eroticism in Part Two, when Jack is described as 'admiring' Arthur Shaw's 'huge back'. Faulks, instead, chooses to concentrate on heterosexual liaisons and their impact on the characters involved. Many of these relationships share common features, such as Jack's marriage to Margaret which has some similarities with the affair between Stephen and Isabelle. They share a similar age-gap, with the women in each case being approximately ten years older than the men. Jack and Margaret have a brief courtship, leading to marriage within three months of their meeting. Stephen and Isabelle, while they do not marry, advance their relationship rapidly and within weeks of meeting, she has left her husband and they have set up home together. Here the similarities end: Jack's marriage is portrayed as stable, loving, warm and close, while Stephen and Isabelle's affair is destructive to everybody concerned. This affair is used to demonstrate Stephen's personality, Isabelle's profound effect upon him and how this impacts on him during the war. His time with her provides him with his first experience of love and yet he cannot completely commit himself to the relationship, or to her. One senses that there is always something missing.

The descriptions of the physical side of Stephen and Isabelle's relationship are similar to the later descriptions of battle wounds. In both cases, Sebastian Faulks pays particular attention to the senses as well as to the impact of wounds and sex upon the flesh. There is great emphasis on various body parts and how they feel and react to the touch, as well as how they look, smell and taste. He also focuses on body fluids, whether this be blood, semen, or saliva. This similarity of language forces the reader to compare these two aspects of Stephen's life, although the links can sometimes feel a little contrived and occasionally obvious - as in the description of the prostitute, when Stephen directly contrasts her body with the shell-damaged flesh of Reeves and Douglas as they lay dead or dying in the trenches.

Despite the vivid descriptions of Stephen and Isabelle's sexual relations, there is also a slight coyness in Faulk's language which gives this section of the novel the air of romantic fiction. Unlike Pat Barker in the *Regeneration Trilogy*, or Sebastian Barry in *A Long Long Way*, Faulks refrains from using colloquial language to describe various parts of human anatomy, but then neither does he use any 'proper' words. So, for example, Stephen's penis is not referred to directly but is called 'his flesh', 'the part of him', 'his gross excitement' and so on. The reason for romanticising their sexual liaison is to give it a greater importance in Stephen's life and in the building of his character. This is not, we are led to believe, just a meaningless 'romp', but a consuming, life-changing experience, which rises above the need for simple words and requires instead lyrical descriptions. Faulks is also reminding the reader of how much Isabelle is giving up when she chooses to leave Stephen and also of the impact of her abandonment upon him. She believes, we are told, that through Stephen she has discovered that she was 'born for this' - for a strong, physically intense relationship with a loving partner, and yet she leaves all of this behind and returns to her family and, eventually, to Azaire. However, these sex scenes fail to really achieve their goal. One can appreciate the importance of Isabelle's presence without knowing, in such great and graphic detail, how every part of her body felt to Stephen's touch. In fact, the description of these events becomes repetitive and mechanical, rather than arousing and passionate.

Stephen's growing friendship, and eventual marriage, to Jeanne is entirely different from his affair with her sister. While there is a haunting element to this earlier union, it is Jeanne's love which eventually saves him. There is no mention of sex between Stephen and Jeanne, which provides a notable contrast between this deep and lasting relationship and his earlier passionate yet destructive affair. Not long after first meeting Jeanne, Stephen contemplates writing to her to explain how important her kindness has become to him, believing that her 'friendship enables me to survive'. He does not send this letter, but even thinking about it proves that she had become very important in his life. This unsent letter contrasts with another, which he also did not send, to his employer in Part One, which spoke of his uncontrollable passion for Isabelle. In this letter he had written that his 'conviction' of his love for Isabelle 'brings me no joy', which shows that, before he had consummated his desires, he already sensed the damaging consequences of their love. Through his relationship with Jeanne, Stephen, it would seem, has begun to learn that love is about much more than sex.

Other First World War novels, which have been written in the latter part of the twentieth century, also feature relationships between men and women, which prove important to the development of characters within the plot. One such example would be Pat Barker's *Regeneration*, which includes a developing liaison between Billy Prior, a troubled patient at Craiglockhart Military Hospital and Sarah Lumb, a strong-minded independent factory worker. Pat Barker has portrayed this relationship in much more harsh and gritty terms than Faulks uses, which reflects her own writing style and the need to portray the fact that Billy is a deeply disturbed young man, whose initial requirement from Sarah is simple: he wants to have sex, and nothing more. Gradually, they grow emotionally closer, but Billy is always reserved. In the second part of the Trilogy, *The Eye In the Door*, Barker's use of language in describing Billy's more adventurous sexual activities, becomes even more coarse and colloquial. This continues in *The Ghost Road*, but it must be said that these descriptions reflect the fact that, for Billy, sex is a means of regaining some control over his own life and affording himself some physical relief, rather than being of emotional significance.

In *A Long Long Way*, Sebastian Barry gives two very different accounts of his central character's sexual exploits. In the first, Willie visits a prostitute in Amiens. Barry gives a detailed description of Willie's actions and reactions to his few moments of pleasure with this girl, which will go on to have disastrous consequences later in the story. Shortly after this event, Willie is granted leave and goes back to Ireland. The evening before he is due to return to France, Gretta, his beloved girlfriend, visits him and there is a clear indication that they make love, although the physical details are left entirely to the reader's imagination in a metaphorical closing of the bedroom door. This is, we are led to believe, a private act between two lovers, the details of which are not relevant. The effect of these two descriptions is to place a greater importance on Willie's brief indiscretion with the prostitute than his long-term relationship with Gretta. Eventually the reason for this becomes clear. Willie did not seem to really enjoy his experience with the prostitute and yet, when Gretta finds out about his infidelity, she abandons him and marries another young man instead, quickly bearing him a child. Thus the reader discovers that Willie's momentary lapse was not only less than pleasurable, but it had a cost which even he could not have contemplated.

There are also some marked similarities in the way Sebastian Faulks and Sebastian Barry have described their characters' visits to prostitutes, although the author's techniques vary. Faulks gives a more detailed and vivid description of the two women, mother and daughter, with whom Stephen eventually fails to have sex. The mother is portrayed in an unfavourable light with the emphasis being placed upon her age. The daughter, on the other hand, is initially given a more glamourous and beautiful depiction, although this is mainly because Stephen marvels at her body which remains undamaged by the war. The comparison which he makes in his own mind, with the bodies of the men who have been wounded preys on his mind, eventually giving rise to a temporary breakdown. Barry also describes his prostitute in terms of her beauty, but in much less flamboyant language. This is a business transaction, to be dealt with accordingly and, although Willie fancies for a brief moment that he is in love with the girl, there are no real emotional ties or remembrances to hinder him. Equally, Faulks has given a full and detailed description of the mother's application of disinfectant to herself. He describes the 'gash between her legs' in great detail, including how it reacts to her touch. This episode is repeated in Barry's novel - but in much less detail. Here, we are not told how the prostitute looks, merely that she applies the disinfectant. In fact, he gives more detail about the 'chipped enamel basin' from which she obtains the liquid, than he does about the girl herself.

In both cases, these methods of describing the respective incidents form a direct relationship with their importance to the characters and the plot. Stephen and Weir's visit to the prostitutes reminds us that, despite the passage of time, Stephen has not really forgotten Isabelle, and also that he is more affected by the sights of war which he has witnessed than we might otherwise have understood. Even his basic need for sexual relief takes second place to his memories. In the case of Willie Dunne's character, the brothel scene is given an air of cheap vulgarity to contrast it with his relationship with Gretta.

Authors who were writing earlier in the twentieth century did not have the same freedom of expression as is granted to modern day writers. They could not mention the physical act of sex, although they could hint at it taking place - or at the desire for it to take place. In *All Quiet on the Western Front*, published in 1929, Erich Maria Remarque describes a visit made by three of his characters to some French women. The men take food to the women, in return for which, the women offer themselves to the three soldiers. While two of the men seem quite happy with this arrangement, Paul Bäumer is initially uncertain, wondering whether his life will always be haunted by memories of war and brothels and if he will ever be able to enjoy being with a woman in normal circumstances. Remarque describes the young woman's face, her foreign words, her reactions as they appear to Paul and also his mixed emotions as she kisses him. Everything else is left entirely to the reader's imagination. We are not told whether they make love, or simply kiss. All we know is that afterwards, Paul is 'not in the least happy'. In all probability, this is because Paul had been looking for an emotional connection, which he had failed to find.

In many of these cases, the vivid descriptions of sex do not add to the plot and in some instances, they even detract from it. The adage that 'less is more' can frequently be applied to sex scenes as the reader's imagination can almost always create a more intense situation than the author could produce. To believe that a character is in love, on the other hand, requires more work on the author's part. In this, almost all of the authors featured above have failed. Stephen, we are told, is in love with Isabelle: he tells her so and, when she abandons him, he pines relentlessly for many years. Yet his actions when they are together force the reader to question his devotion. His upbringing and background make it difficult for him to commit himself to anyone, so perhaps this is the best he has to offer, but somehow, it always seems that he is holding something back. In *A Long Long Way*, Willie Dunne's relationship with Gretta Lawlor is so scantily and quickly described that it is difficult to truly believe that he manages to form so deep an attachment to her. In addition, his love is never really reciprocated as Gretta never really gives Willie any reason to hope that they have a future together, so the reader wonders why he has such high expectations. Neither does a loving relationship really seem to exist between Billy Prior and Sarah Lumb, in Pat Barker's *Regeneration*. Admittedly, this central characters is being portrayed as a confused and deeply disturbed young man, whose reactions can rightly be expected to be out of the ordinary. Even given this perspective, however, Pat Barker's central character, who, like Stephen Wraysford, claims to be in love, behaves in ways which can only lead to the destruction of both his, and Sarah's happiness. Ironically, in most cases, where the authors have succeeded in describing the sensation of love, it is not the conventional love of a man for a woman, but the bonds of comradeship formed in the trenches, where we are often shown the true depths of a man's feelings and his commitment to another person, made complete by their shared experiences and earnest emotional ties.

3. PORTRAYAL OF THE HOME FRONT

In *Birdsong*, we are given two separate portrayals of the home front, both of which depict civilians in an unfavourable light. During Weir's visit to his parents, which is only briefly and retrospectively described, we discover that they are callously oblivious to the danger in which their son lives, and that they are not at all interested in listening to him. This representation says as much about Weir's character as it does about the home front. His difficulty in forming relationships with women makes more sense, when one realises that there is little affection between him and his parents. He is not used to either giving or receiving tenderness, which makes his friendship with Stephen even more poignant.

The story of Weir's time at home is told from his own perspective, in hindsight and in anger at his parent's reactions to him and to the war. His telegram has failed to forewarn his parents of his arrival and his father initially seems more interested in feeding a toad in his greenhouse, than in greeting his son. He also seems unsure as to whether Weir will even be staying at the family home, although it seems clear that he has nowhere else to go. His mother's attitude is no better as, although she shows concern at his loss of weight and is pleased that he is 'all in one piece', she allows him to sit alone in the dining room eating his hastily prepared meal, rather than keeping him company. Weir's father is certain that he has all the information he could possibly need from the newspapers and is not at all keen to hear his son's version, even though Weir is clearly desperate to talk. By the time Weir returns to France, he claims that he would be happy to see 'a five-day bombardment on their street'.

Stephen Wraysford also has a spell of leave in England, during which he also experiences complacency and arrogance, even 'resentment' from the civilians with whom he comes into contact, with the notable exception of a woman on a train, who offers to telephone his family. However, during this leave, Stephen finds himself at peace for the first time in many years. He is able to look at the world with the eyes of forgiveness and finds that he has more optimism for the future. The narrative here forces the reader to compare the English countryside with the wasted land of France which Stephen has so recently vacated. This somewhat contrived description of Stephen's self-revelation also contrasts with the callous conceit of almost all of the civilians in this section of the story, showing perhaps that to Stephen it has now become apparent that the land itself is more worthy than its inhabitants.

Even novels which are set entirely on the home front, continue with this portrayal of complacency and arrogance. Rebecca West's *The Return of the Soldier*, published in 1918, tells the story of a single family - Chris Baldry, his wife, Kitty and cousin Jenny. Chris has lost his memory and believes himself to be 21 years old and still in a relationship with his first love, Margaret. The three women in the story must decide whether to allow Chris to remain in blissful oblivion or to disillusion him and let him return to the dangers of war. Jenny is initially undecided. Margaret wants whatever is best for Chris, but believes that he should be kept safe at all costs and eventually Jenny comes to agree with her. These two women are portrayed as caring individuals. Kitty, Chris's wife, on the other hand, is determined that nothing should be allowed to affect her well-ordered life and insists that Chris should be forced to return to reality, regardless of the cost to himself. West's portrayal of Kitty is so unfavourable that the reader cannot fail to find her attitude unacceptable. She is shown to be arrogant and selfish in the extreme, placing her own needs and desires ahead of everything else. She will not listen to anyone - even the doctor whom she has summoned to 'cure' her husband. Nothing is to be allowed to stand in the way of her happiness - even her husband's death, it would seem, would be more acceptable than for him to continue to live a lie. Such an obvious portrayal makes the reader automatically sympathise with Chris, as well as Jenny and Margaret.

Similarly, Pat Barker's *Regeneration* shows civilians in a less than flattering light. Generally speaking, she depicts them as exploiting the war, trying to make out of it whatever they can. In addition, life on the home front is shown as continuing pretty much as before the war, forcing Billy Prior to question whether people even realise that the war is going on. The exception to this is Sarah Lumb. Admittedly, she has left her job as a servant, to work in a munitions factory because she gets paid more, but also because she has always resent having to be subservient to others. However, her attitude to the wounded soldiers she discovers at the hospital, shows that she is not uncaring towards them. Indeed, she is angered by the fact that they are hidden away and also resents the fact that their heroism is not publicly acknowledged. In revealing her anger to Billy, she helps to cement their relationship as he begins to see her in a new and more positive light.

In looking at *Birdsong*, it is clear that neither Weir nor Stephen feel that they really belong at home anymore, although in Stephen's case this is not surprising, being as he had lived in France for four years, prior to the beginning of the war. Nonetheless, this feeling of being an outsider is one which is popularly represented in the fiction of the First World War. In *All Quiet on the Western Front*, Paul Bäumer's leave is spoiled by the feeling that he does not fit in. He has no-one to talk to, as they are not interested in hearing what he has to say; his possessions, especially his books, which had once seemed so important to him, now seem insignificant. These changes of perspective show us that the soldiers themselves had changed, while at home, everything had remained the same. Unlike Weir, however, Paul Bäumer does not become angry about the complacency of those at home: he longs to return to the front to be amongst true friends and adopts an attitude of quiet, bemused acceptance of the situation at home.

Susan Hill's *Strange Meeting* also covers this aspect of disassociation with one's former home life. The novel opens with John Hilliard's convalescent leave coming to an end and his relief at being able to leave the stifling environment of his family home and return to the front, is palpable. In a similar style to that used by Sebastian Faulks, Susan Hill has given Hilliard's home life an air of emotional detachment. His mother, Constance, is more concerned with the family's appearance than with her son's wellbeing. She is a woman who is not used to showing her emotions and she expects her children to behave in a similar fashion. The reason for this portrayal is two-fold, and comparable to Faulks's representation of Weir's upbringing. In both cases, the men involved find it difficult to form friendships. Weir, unfortunately never really gets the opportunity and his dependency on Wraysford is the closest he comes to a close attachment. This disappoints the reader as one feels that his character has so much more to offer. In the case of Hilliard, however, his attachment and eventual declaration of love for his fellow officer, David Barton - a man from a large, loving and openly demonstrative family - shows how Hilliard has learned to love and to be loved by someone else. The fact that he learns this through the friendship of another man is irrelevant, but somehow, more affecting.

Due to the fact that most of the novels about the First World War are written from the perspective of the soldiers - and especially the officers - of the time, the home front has tended to be a neglected and misrepresented area. In most cases, these authors fail to convey the concept that the home front and the trenches represent two entirely different worlds, both of which were harsh in their own way, but neither of which really understood the other. In reality, the home front was not embodied by complacent, arrogant, selfish, opportunists, but by people struggling, just as the soldiers were, to come to terms with the devastation of their lives and their society. While almost everyone accepted that the men at the front were suffering the worst fate of all, it has to be realised that on the home front, children were dying from the effects of malnutrition. Others were placed into orphanages because their mothers could not cope, or had occasionally committed suicide. Women were frequently working in factories, in hospitals and on farms, for long hours and then going home to their 'wifely' or 'motherly' duties. Many mothers work today, but we have labour-saving gadgets which were not afforded to this earlier generation. In addition, there was always the dreaded knock on the door of the postman (or, quite often, woman), or telegraph boy, bringing the long-feared news of death, or injury. In many cases, a death in the family not only meant the loss of a loved one, but the depletion of the household income, which in many cases, had far reaching consequences. Generally speaking, people were more emotionally repressed than they are today, preferring to remain silent in their grief or thoughts than to speak about them. This refers not only to soldiers, but to civilians, many of whom never spoke of their losses. Men, especially the older generation, found it difficult to accept the loss of their sons, when there was nothing which they could do themselves.

All Quiet on the Home Front by Richard Van Emden and Steve Humphries gives first-hand accounts of life on the home front during the First World War, showing how stereotypical some representations of civilians in literature can be. Fictional recreations, such as those portrayed in *Birdsong*, are used to make the reader even more sympathetic towards the main, combatant characters.

4. THE DEPICTION OF BATTLE SCENES

The creation of strong, realistic battle scenes is something for which Sebastian Faulks's *Birdsong* has been considered, by many, to be noteworthy. As the men await the beginning of the Battle of the Somme, Faulks begins by creating and air of tension, as the soldiers are sent into the trenches, only to be told that they must wait for an additional two days. This supposed 'reprieve' only serves to make them more apprehensive, especially when they discover that, rather than attacking at dawn, they are to advance in daylight. What follows in the battle itself, is a description of blind chaos, gruesome wounding and death, faltering progress and pointlessness. Faulks creates the battle scene in great detail, depicting Stephen's perspective of the experience, telling us his thoughts and reactions to the situation. The language in these scenes is uncompromisingly harsh but also, occasionally, poetic. For instance, Faulks describes a dead man's intestines 'slopped out on the scooped soil of the shellhole where the sun began to bake it'; he also says 'He was running, raging, in a dream, downhill, towards the river' and 'Skylarks wheeled and sang high in the cloudless sky'. The use of lyrical and graphic language, as well as alliteration and assonance in these passages gives them an air of detachment from the reality of battle which compliments Stephen's sense that what is happening is unnatural and unbelievable, mingled with his occasional feelings of being more of an observer than a participant.

In addition to the passages which describe Stephen's involvement in the battle, there is also an account of the scene as it appears to observers. Jack Firebrace, Arthur Shaw and the Padré, Horrocks, watch the unfolding battle from an advantage point behind the lines and wonder at the unmitigated slaughter which is happening before them, but which they are powerless to prevent. Rather than responding to the scenes described here, the reader focuses on the reactions of these three men, all of whom behave differently. Arthur Shaw, weeping and calling out to 'my poor boys' is probably the most poignant and thought-provoking of these reactions, as he is a hardened soldier, who has seen a great deal of action and yet he is moved to tears by the sights before him. In addition, the post-battle roll-call is noteworthy. Many of the names which are called out and fail to produce a response, are characters with whom the reader has become familiar. Price, a seasoned campaigner, cannot enquire after every man and simply reads the list of names verbatim. More than three-quarters of the men are dead, wounded or missing and those who remain are shattered by what they have experienced. Sebastian Faulks delivers this information in a relatively matter-of-fact manner, pausing to mention the impact which these deaths will have on those at home.

Within these relatively short passages, Faulks has managed to convey four different perspectives of battle: the participant, the observer, the survivor and the family left behind. In each case his language, once again, leaves little to the imagination. We are spared none of the detail, none of the emotion or consequences of war, but are left feeling drained by the experience.

Many authors within this genre, also portray battle scenes. Susan Hill's novel *Strange Meeting*, is predominantly concerned with the meeting of two young men, John Hilliard and David Barton, and the consequences of their relationship. However, during the course of the novel, they are required to go into battle and here we can see a very different description of the scene. Susan Hill does not use such harsh language as Sebastian Faulks, although she still manages to convey the chaos and destruction of battle. When she tells us that a man has 'his chest and stomach half torn away', that is the extent of her description. There is no need to tell us any more than that, because the main concern here is that the man in question is Parkin, a minor character, but one who gives his life in an attempt to save John Hilliard. Due to the nature of this novel, the reader is more concerned with Hilliard's reaction to this death and with his urgent need, despite his own injuries, to get back to the trenches and discover the fate of David Barton. So, although the battle scenes are important and are given due explanation, they are not the main point of interest here.

Where both *Birdsong* and *Strange Meeting* could be said to suffer is in the narrative viewpoint of these two novels. Both are told in the third person. In Birdsong, the parts of the story which relate to the war are told essentially from the perspective of Stephen Wraysford. *Strange Meeting*, on the other hand, has a more 'all-seeing', or omniscient, narrator. In this respect, nothing which happens can really be seen to shock or surprise the characters involved, leaving the reader to feel that they are witnessing the battles, rather than participating in them. An alternative description can be found in Erich Maria Remarque's *All Quiet on the Western Front*, which is told in the first person and the present tense. Unlike Sebastian Faulks and Susan Hill, Remarque was writing from experience, having served in the German army on the Western Front during 1917. Here, he was wounded, when a shell fragment hit him in the leg and he was not passed fit for action again until just before the end of the war. Remarque, in Chapter Six of his novel, creates an atmosphere of tension as the young German soldiers sit in a dugout, under a massive bombardment, awaiting an anticipated attack. The claustrophobia and miserable fear of this situation are captured perfectly. Some of the less experienced soldiers begin to 'rave' at the unrelenting noise and try to escape from the dugout. The central character and narrator, Paul Bäumer, chases after one man, but a shell scores a direct hit and Paul finds himself facing a wall of 'smoking splinters, lumps of flesh, and bits of uniform.'

The element of fear is captured in a much more realistic fashion because it is Paul himself who is telling the story. This can be seen when comparing Paul's assertion that: 'Our legs refuse to move, our hands tremble, our bodies are a thin skin stretched painfully over repressed madness', with Faulks's 'He walked hesitatingly forward, his skin tensed for the feeling of metal tearing flesh'. The latter statement evokes a sense of dread, but the tone is less enthralling than in the first excerpt. The tense of the piece is of importance here, as writing in the present tense has helped Remarque create a greater sense of urgency in his piece.

Remarque's descriptions of wounds are, if anything, more realistic than those in *Birdsong*. Paul, an already experienced soldier, although he is not yet twenty, witnesses the carnage of battle almost in slow-motion. He tells us of a man who has his 'head torn off', but still manages to take a few more paces, 'while the blood spouts from his neck like a fountain.' One can see similarities between this description and those which Sebastian Faulks has employed in his battle scenes.

Another difference between these two interpretations of battle is the thought processes through which the central characters are shown to pass. Stephen Wraysford seems to find the time to think about all sorts of things including how abhorrent the world has become; that everything has become 'profane'; that the world has 'been dislocated'. Paul Bäumer, on the other hand, spares no time for sermonising, but focuses on surviving, no matter how much of a 'wild beast' this means he must become: he will fight and kill in order to survive. Only later, when the battle has ceased, does Paul pause to think. Even then, however, he does not wonder at what has become of the world, or question the tactics or reasons behind the war. Instead he focuses on his past and whether he will ever again experience peace and if he does, will he ever be able to live a normal life again?

Memoirs of the First World War sometimes give another type of battle description, which is surprisingly matter-of-fact. In *The Last of the Ebb*, for example, Sidney Rogerson describes a dead body as follows: '... something twisted and shapeless which had once been a man, had been blown like a bundle of old brown paper on to the grass.' Rather than focusing on the man's wounds or appearance, Rogerson instead recalls how this recently killed body gave him a message, 'as plainly as any signpost': namely that the area in which he had found himself was likely to be dangerous and that it was advisable to vacate the scene as quickly as possible! Many memoirs, such as this one, recall battles from the perspective of military manoeuvres, rather than as scenes of death and destruction. This may be for the obvious reason that it was preferable for the authors not to remember every single detail. Alternatively, it could signify how difficult it was, in the heat of battle, to actually recall how many deaths one witnessed and what form they took - simply because there were so many.

Water-filled trench at
Passchendaele, 1917.

Ruins of Ypres seen from the air.

Germans in Bapaume ruins during the Battle of
the Somme.
Photo by Robert Carlson.

Images courtesy of gwpda.org.

CRITICAL ANALYSIS

1. THE STRUCTURE OF THE NOVEL

Birdsong is a novel set in seven separate and very different parts. The first, and most frequently criticised of these is set in France in 1910, four years before the beginning of the war. Many students - and other readers - struggle to understand the need for this section of the novel, and some fail to even complete it! The purpose of Part One is to set the scene, build characters, introduce settings and create an atmosphere. In addition, it is necessary - given that Sebastian Faulks wished to tell part of the story in a retrospective fashion, as Elizabeth Benson discovers her ancestry - that Stephen Wraysford should have a child - otherwise there would be no-one to delve into the past, or to complete the story. Parts Two, Four and Six tell the story of Stephen's war. The reader meets many other characters in these sections, only a few of whom survive. Each of them serves a different purpose in the story, but all share a knowledge, however large or small, of Stephen's character. Parts Three, Five and Seven portray Elizabeth's search for understanding, coupled with the effects of her own adulterous affair and pregnancy. These parts of the novel allow the reader to fill in the gaps creating, eventually, a whole picture.

Part One of the novel is told in a fairly conventional and cohesive 'story' format. Stephen and Isabelle meet, fall in love and then separate. In between, they do a fair amount of emotional damage to themselves and to others, have quite a lot of sex and Isabelle, not surprisingly, becomes pregnant. There are several purposes behind the telling of this romance. It helps the reader to understand Stephen Wraysford's character and reactions. If the story of this affair had been told retrospectively, through Stephen's memories, a diary or letters, for example, it would not have been so realistic or meaningful to the reader. The creation of an atmosphere of intense emotion, indulgence and passion shows the depth of feeling of which Stephen is capable, but which he chooses to no longer portray, once he is in the trenches. Stephen's clear desire for Isabelle, which we are led to believe, knows no bounds, is contrasted with his attitude towards sex in the later parts of the novel. He is capable of intercourse with the prostitute and the subject of sex does not seem to arise in his relationship with Jeanne. The war, as well as his doomed affair with Isabelle, have taken their toll on him physically, psychologically and emotionally, to the point where this part of his character has changed beyond recognition.

In addition, this romance provides a contrast with the later affair between Elizabeth and Robert. Their situation is similar to that of Stephen and Isabelle, but after the passage of sixty years, no-one really seems to object to adultery in the same way as they did in 1910. In this way, the reader is made to understand how much times have changed. There is also a link here between Elizabeth and her grandfather, in that both of them could be said to be selfish and inconsiderate. Equally Robert and Isabelle seem to be only concerned with their own feelings and happiness, paying little attention to the effects of their indiscretions.

Another purpose of Part One is to introduce the geographical area in which the war will later take place and to compare its appearance in 1910 with the war-torn landscape of France, six years later. The description of the boat trip on the River Somme, including the mention of 'trenches', 'wooden boarding', 'heavy flies', and rotting, decayed vegetation, is redolent of the battle scenes which will later take place alongside the banks of this river. In addition, the train journey which Stephen and Isabelle take as they flee from Amiens, initially follows a route in which many later battle scenes are mentioned, such as the Marne, the Meuse and Verdun, once again providing links between this part of the story and that which is to follow.

Isabelle's pregnancy - as well as mirroring Elizabeth's later in the novel - also provides the necessary conduit through whom the story can eventually be told. Without the birth of Françoise, there would be no Elizabeth to portray these later parts of the novel. In addition, it is necessary that Isabelle and Stephen cannot remain together. Their passion is too intense to last and

Isabelle's guilt is so destructive, that the reader senses that they must part, almost before they have begun their affair. However, the child must be born, and Isabelle must leave, in order that Stephen may become the isolated character whom Faulks wishes to create and, later, redeem. The manner and reasoning behind her departure, however, is poorly explained and feels rushed and contrived, leaving the reader feeling almost as confused as Stephen.

Part Two of the novel starts with Jack Firebrace under the ground, performing his tasks as a tunneller. There is no mention of Stephen for some time, but when there is, we are immediately made aware of the changes which he has undergone physically and emotionally since we last met him. Other characters are rapidly introduced and, being as the war has been under way for two years, they are all familiar with one another. One of the main reasons that these war-time parts of the novel work better than the others, is that the war is 'dipped into'. We join half way through, and never seem to spend more than a few days with any group or individual, before moving on. In this way, both the novel and the war itself, seem to move apace. Rather than describing the times of monotony, when the men were waiting for something to happen, or giving great long descriptions of Stephen's recovery from his wounds, the story skips forward to more interesting and action-packed scenes.

Within the war sections of the novel, the men are portrayed on leave - both in England and France. They are also depicted, briefly, at rest behind the lines, visiting estaminets and organising small entertainments or taking baths. In each case, however, there is a secondary purpose to these portrayals. Leave in England is used to show the callous indifference of the civilians in question; Stephen's leave in France allows him to be briefly reunited with Isabelle and, more importantly, to meet Jeanne. Time spent behind the lines allows the reader to experience the camaraderie between the men, while the baths help to remind us of the appalling conditions in which they were expected to live. Each of these aspects also helps to create or define the characters involved. So, for example, Weir's visit to England tells us as much about him as it does about the home front. He is nervous and distressed, even when away from the fighting, but we can also see his strained relationship with his parents, compared with his more open and friendly exchanges with Stephen.

Throughout Parts Two, Four and Six, we can see the gradual psychological deterioration of the men. Stephen and Weir both depend on alcohol from the first time we meet them in the trenches, but this dependency - especially in Weir - becomes more marked as the story progresses. Brennan's character is introduced as a relatively simple and contented man, who gains satisfaction at returning his brother's dismembered body to the British trenches, so that he can be buried - thus giving Brennan somewhere to focus his grief after the war. This, we later learn, is a false hope as Brennan's war experiences leave him so damaged that he lives for the rest of his life in a home, disillusioned and detached from reality. These portrayals of the breaking down of the men's spirits, together with Faulks's vivid descriptions of the wounded and dying, all help to illustrate the effects of the First World War on the combatants.

In Part Six, Faulks creates additional tension around Stephen's character, with a 'will he or won't he live' plotline. However, the reader already knows that Stephen survives the war, so this seems unnecessary and fails to build the required sense of apprehension. In addition, the reader is aware that Stephen's rescuer is German and the brother of a man for whose death Stephen had been responsible. Their embrace at the end of this part of the novel seems forced but is necessary to show the element of forgiveness which Stephen has finally learned.

Parts Three, Five and Seven, the modern sections, have the function of completing the story - in every sense - but other than that, serve no purpose. Part Three is set in 1978, sixty years after the end of the First World War, at which time, most of the combatants would have been in their eighties - old and frail, but there would still be some left alive for Elizabeth Benson to discover on her quest to discover the truth. Setting the modern sections any later than this would have given Sebastian Faulks the problem that there would have been far fewer survivors to recount snippets of Stephen's war experiences. Elizabeth's sudden and unexplained interest in her ancestry provides an excuse to delve into her grandfather's past and, through his notebooks, discover more about the war and his part in it. She also decides to travel to France to see the places where he had been and, in doing so, the reader is reminded (especially through her visit to the memorial at Thiepval), how many men perished and were never found in the battleground which surrounded the River Somme.

Within these sections of the novel, the reader can sense that Faulks has used some very obvious links by which he can, very neatly, complete the circular motion of his story. For example, Elizabeth runs a clothing company, while Stephen had worked in the weaving industry; Elizabeth has an affair with a married man, while Stephen had seduced Isabelle under her husband's roof. The language used throughout is similar, so that the birth scene in the final part of the novel, mirrors the fear, panic and bloodiness of the earlier trench settings. The endings of Parts Six and Seven are also very similar. Stephen experiences an 'exultation of his soul' as he begins to come to terms with having survived the war; Robert has a similar feeling as he walks in the garden, following the birth of his son.

Other references are equally contrived and obvious. Many of the different sections of the novel are directly linked to the preceding one. So, Part Three opens in an underground 'tunnel' - providing a connection with Jack Firebrace, who had helped to build the London Underground. The man in the underground train sings 'Tipperary' - a popular song amongst the soldiers in the First World War - and yet is described as a 'mad man'. Part Five ends with Elizabeth reading a translation of one of the entries in Stephen's notebook, while Part Six opens with him putting away his pen and notebook. In addition, by giving birth to a son, Elizabeth is able to fully complete the circle and fulfil Stephen's promise to Jack Firebrace - naming her baby John, in memory of Jack's dead son.

The three modern parts of the story, as a narrative tool, allow the reader to discover the whole story about Stephen's life at the same time as Elizabeth's character. This is, however, somewhat clumsy. For example, there are too many contrived similarities between her life and her grandfather's; too many obvious reminders of the First World War - a conflict about which Elizabeth is remarkably ignorant and her astonishingly sudden interest in her ancestry is not sufficiently explained to make sense within the plot - making this element feel manufactured.

Sebastian Faulks has also made use of other narrative instruments to tell the story, including letters. These are used to illustrate the thoughts of the writers or for them to create an impression as to how they feel, to the recipient. Stephen's feelings for Isabelle are first revealed in an unsent letter to his company. Jack Firebrace's reaction to the death of his son, as demonstrated in his letters, is one of gratitude and slightly withheld sorrow. It is only when he faces his own death that we can see his real feelings for his son. Weir, on the other hand, writes an unrealistically optimistic letter to his parents on the eve of the Battle of the Somme. In this, he essentially tells them what he thinks they want to hear, rather than the truth. His letter ends formally and suddenly, following Weir's request that 'no more socks or pullovers' should be sent out to him. Tipper's letter, which immediately follows this one, is altogether different. He explains that he finds the 'waiting awful hard', but urges his family not to worry about him. Although this letter ends in a similar fashion to Weir's, the preceding sentences are full of affection for his family.

Letters serve another purpose, namely as a form of narration. From Tipper's letter we can learn that he has recovered from his hysteria and been returned to his unit; that Byrne has been kind to him; that the men were ignorant of the reality of the situation, in that they believed they would face 'no resistance' from the Germans. Weir's letter, similarly tells us that the tunnellers have finished their work and will have no official active role in the battle, although some of them have volunteered as stretcher bearers. Wraysford's letter to Isabelle is different again. Here Faulks paints a more general picture of the war, informing us that the forthcoming battle is, in Wraysford's opinion, going to be seen as a 'crime against nature'. These letters, therefore allow the reader to understand the enormity of the task ahead of the men, as well as the minutiae of the individuals' lives.

2. LANGUAGE

Throughout the novel, Sebastian Faulks makes use of poetic language and tools to create atmosphere and give his descriptions more power and imagination. He also uses symbolic language to subliminally inform or remind the reader of certain points of interest. An example of this can be seen right at the beginning of the novel in the description of the house in which the Azaire family live. Faulks tells us that it is a 'strong, formal' building, behind which hide 'unseen footsteps'. These descriptions afford the house similar qualities to its owners, namely strength and mystery, but also imply hidden intrigues. This immediately telegraphs that something secretive may be about to happen within the walls of this building.

Creating realistic tension or atmosphere is vital in a novel of this type, where the reader could otherwise never hope to fully understand the motivations behind the actions of the characters involved. Faulks achieves this in several sections of the novel, most notably during the boat trip on the River Somme, where he creates a sultry, sensuous, indulgent atmosphere, in which the tension between Isabelle and Stephen becomes almost too great for them to tolerate. In addition, he adds to this by introducing elements which will later relate to the First World War, and in doing so, ensures that when the reader reaches those sections, we will be reminded of the earlier scenes.

In Part Three, Faulks describes the 'train of the Central Line [which] fitted its tube like a bullet in the barrel of a rifle', this simile links the London Underground with the armaments of battle. He also reminds us that the tunnels of the Underground were 'dug by sweating tunnellers' which is reminiscent of Jack Firebrace's role before and during the war. Later, Faulks uses familiarity to spark the reader's imagination, in his description of the Star and Garter home. He recounts the decor, the colour of the door, the flooring and brickwork, the lighting and even the aromas which emit from the kitchens, although these are soon overpowered by the smell of disinfectant. This all paints a rather depressing picture of the place in which Brennan has spent the last sixty years of his life, forcing the reader to remember his role in the war scenes and reminding us how much the modern characters take for granted in their relatively luxurious lifestyles.

In addition, there are several instances where the reader may relate Faulks's language in the novel directly to some of the poetry of the First World War. These include a reference, in Part Two, to Douglas 'pouring himself away', as Stephen remembers the soldier's bloody death in the trenches. This statement is reminiscent of two First World War poems. Firstly, in *Disabled*, Wilfred Owen mentions that the maimed subject of his poem had 'poured [his blood] down shell-holes'. Secondly, Rupert Brooke's *The Dead* (i), tells us of men who have 'poured out the red/Sweet wine of youth'. Both poets and Faulks are reminding their readers that these men did not choose to pour away their blood, but have done so metaphorically, in that the war has forced them to waste their lives.

The scenes underground, especially when Stephen is trapped with Jack Firebrace and then rescued by Levi, are reminiscent of Owen's *Strange Meeting*. In this poem, Owen describes an encounter between two soldiers from opposing sides. They meet, essentially, in Hell, although Owen describes this as simply an underground tunnel. The eventual meeting between Wraysford and Levi echoes this poem, in that the opposing soldiers cannot blame or hate one another for earlier actions, as both of them are just grateful for peace.

The language which surrounds the deaths of certain characters varies greatly and this variation is occasionally inconsistent. Normally more important characters would have a greater description afforded to their deaths, but in *Birdsong*, this is not always the case. Ellis's death for example, is only referred to briefly with the information that he had been 'killed by machine-gun fire'. Ellis plays quite an important role, emphasising to the reader how war-weary both Weir and Wraysford have become, and yet his death is glossed-over. Earlier, the wounds and eventual deaths of Douglas, Wilkinson and Reeves are described in great detail, with full information provided as to how they received their injuries. Weir's death is treated differently again, in that the description here is more poetic, almost as though it is happening in slow-motion. There is some significance in this, as Weir's last encounter with Stephen had resulted with his friend angrily pushing him face-down in the mud. This description allows the reader to understand the importance of this action, as it is mirrored in his death.

Quite often, however, authors give more vivid descriptions of the deaths of less important characters, as the more important ones are simply too significant. It is enough just to know that that character is dead, so we do not need to understand the details surrounding his death. Sebastian Faulks varies his accounts of different characters' deaths, to the point where some are barely noticeable. The suicide of Barnes, for instance, is dealt with in one sentence as we are simply told that, while waiting for the Battle of the Somme to commence, he 'shot himself through the palate'. In this way, such deaths become as commonplace as the author intends. By not focusing on them, neither does the reader and these events take on, therefore, less significance. That is not to say that Faulks is implying that the deaths of the men were not important, but that there were so many of them, he could not possibly give an equal amount of description to each one.

The earth settles following the explosion of the mine beneath Hawthorn Ridge Redoubt on 1st July, 1916.
Photographer: (assumed to be) Lt. Ernest Brooks.
Copyright: Crown copyright.

HISTORICAL SIGNIFICANCE

1. BATTLE OF THE SOMME

The Battle of the Somme is probably the most famous, or infamous, battle of the First World War and its name has become synonymous with the mass destruction of human lives that typified the conflict.

The decision to attack at this particular point on the Western Front was taken, reluctantly, by Sir Douglas Haig, the Commander in Chief of the British Forces. He would have preferred to mount an offensive in Flanders. Initial plans were that the operation would be mounted jointly by the French and British armies but the German attack at Verdun tied up substantial numbers of French troops, meaning that the Somme became a mainly British affair. The French urged Haig to begin the attack as early as possible, bringing the start date forward by one month, to relieve the pressure on their troops at Verdun and divert German resources from that attack.

The artillery bombardment which preceded the attack lasted seven days. The ferocity of this bombardment was intended to destroy the German barbed wire and defences, enabling the attacking force to advance unimpeded. This failed: the German defences were much more solidly built than anticipated; many of the British munitions failed to explode and therefore the wire was, to all intents and purposes, intact.

The British also exploded 17 mines along the German front. However, one of these (at Hawthorn Ridge) was detonated ten minutes before the main attack, giving the Germans sufficient warning and enabling them to prepare for the anticipated onslaught. The element of surprise was lost.

The battle began at 7.30am on the 1st July 1916. Men climbed out of the trenches and, laden down with equipment, walked across No-Man's Land. The reason they were told to walk, rather than run, was because, for many of the men, this was their first experience of battle. The commanding officers hoped, therefore, that greater discipline would be maintained if the men were walking in regimented lines, rather than running at different paces. However, they were an easy target for the German machine gunners. Nearly 60,000 Allied soldiers became casualties that day, of which 20,000 were killed. The first day of the Battle of the Somme became - and remains - the bloodiest in British military history.

The battle dragged on until November 18th 1916, and in total (including Commonwealth, French and German forces) cost over one million lives. The memorial at Thiepval commemorates the missing of the Somme. On its walls are carved the names of over 73,000 men from the United Kingdom and South Africa who have no known grave.

2. BATTLE OF MESSINES

The object of this attack was the capture of the German stronghold of Messines Ridge, southeast of Ypres. Launched on June 7th 1917, this battle preceded the Third Battle of Ypres (also known as Passchendaele) which started at the end of July. The success of the Passchendaele offensive depended heavily on the capture of Messines Ridge, which was also used as a diversionary tactic to prevent the Germans realising that a greater attack was planned.

One of the main features of this battle was the detonation of nineteen mines along the German front immediately before the commencement of the battle. Learning from the mistakes of the Somme, the Germans were given no time to recover themselves before the onslaught began. In fact approximately 10,000 Germans were killed in the explosions alone. The sound of these mines exploding could be heard in both London and Dublin.

With such diminished resistance, Allied troops were able to take and hold Messines Ridge despite several German counter-attacks.

COURSEWORK ASSISTANCE

The coursework element of A-Level study involves the student reading, understanding and interpreting their chosen text; analysing the way in which the writer has used structure, form and language to achieve their purpose; comparing or connecting it to other texts within this genre and demonstrating an understanding of the context in which the text has been set. In this section I have attempted to provide some assistance for students who are using this novel as part of their coursework. In the first section, I provide some suggestions for essay titles and content for the prose element of coursework studies. In the second section, I will look at using *Birdsong* as a comparison with some of the plays of the First World War.

1. ESSAY SUGGESTIONS

PERSONAL INFORMED INTERPRETATION

Students who decide to write this type of essay should be aware of what is meant by the term 'personal informed interpretation'. Think of this phrase as three separate words:

'Personal' - What does the novel mean to *you*? How does it make *you* feel? This does not have to be a positive feeling - just because someone you know loves this novel above all others, does not mean that you have to! However, do not just write your essay in the form of a 'rant' - your reasons, whether you love or loathe the novel, must be reasoned and reasonable, but above all, personal.

'Informed' - Your essay must demonstrate that you have understood the novel. In addition, you will be required to endorse this understanding with wider, relevant reading, showing that you have selected and studied appropriate texts in order to support your arguments.

'Interpretation' - You need to explain your understanding. In other words, you cannot just write 'When Sebastian Faulks says 'He felt himself grow cold', he is telling us that Stephen has become isolated from his environment', and leave it at that. You must go on to explore Stephen's isolation; how it came about; how his experiences with Isabelle affect the rest of his life; why these experiences meant so much to him. So, whatever topic you have chosen to discuss or explore in your essay, you should show that you have thought about the subject in hand and reasoned through your explanations, reinforcing these with highly relevant and specific references to the text.

Birdsong lends itself mainly to essays which focus on themes, structure, language, or characters. Students need to choose a task which enables them to answer all of the assessment objectives required, concisely and accurately, demonstrating that they have understood the text. The following are just a few suggestions for possible essay titles and content, together with ideas for specific further reading:

(a) 'Explore the portrayal of male relationships in *Birdsong*.'

- Here the student should pay attention to the friendship between Weir and Wraysford and could compare this, briefly, with Wraysford's dealings with other characters in the novel.

- Examine how each of these two characters treats the other. Weir seems to depend more on Wraysford than on anyone else, while Wraysford appears more independent. Weir's death, however, changes the readers perspective of their friendship.

- Stephen's notebook is used by Faulks to demonstrate his innermost thoughts and it is noteworthy that in this, Stephen seems to focus on Weir and the other men who have died.

- Reading other novels in this genre would enable students to see how different authors have dealt with this topic. Good examples can be found in *All Quiet on the Western Front* (Erich Maria Remarque) and *Strange Meeting* (Susan Hill).

- How realistic is this friendship? Today, two heterosexual men would be more than reluctant to admit to such an extremely close friendship, but in the First World War, such relationships were not at all unusual. Good references for this context can be found in *1914-1918: Voices and Images of the Great War* or *1915: The Death of Innocence*, both by Lyn MacDonald or *Forgotten Voices of the Great War* by Max Arthur.

Additional information and guidance on this topic, both in *Birdsong* and other novels, can be found in this Study Guide, in the Chapter entitled *Themes and Comparisons - Male Relationships*.

(b) 'Explore the portrayal of love in *Birdsong*.'

- Within this topic, one could examine Stephen Wraysford's liaisons with Isabelle and Jeanne.

- Explore how these two relationships are portrayed by Sebastian Faulks. The first is clearly a passionate, intense and sexual affair, with far-reaching consequences for everyone involved. The second, while more calm and chaste, is no less important and it is Jeanne with whom Stephen spends the rest of his life.

- Focus on Faulks's use of language in describing these two relationships - not just in his descriptions of what actually happens, but in how he shows the characters reactions to each other and the events surrounding them.

- Look at the emotions of each woman towards Stephen. Jeanne feels concern and pity, which deepen into love. Isabelle feels desire and love, which changes into guilt. There are many reasons why their feelings change. See the chapter in this study guide which focuses on *Characters* for a more detailed explanation.

- To examine the portrayal of heterosexual love in other novels in this genre, one could look at *A Long Long Way* (Sebastian Barry).

- How authentic are these relationships to the time in which they are set? If you remove the lurid sexual descriptions of the affair between Isabelle and Stephen, then this scenario is perfectly feasible. Reading any literature of the time - or earlier - demonstrates that adultery is not a modern invention. Jeanne's relationship with Stephen is equally understandable in the context, given its beginnings and its slow progression. In writing about love and relationships in the context of war, one should always remember the temptation to 'seize the day', rather than moralise from a 21st century perspective.

Additional information and guidance on this topic, both in *Birdsong* and other novels, can be found in this Study Guide, in the Chapter entitled *Themes and Comparisons - Portrayal of Love and Sex*.

(c) 'Explore the portrayal of battle scenes in *Birdsong*.'

- Remember that, in reality, most of the time spent in the trenches, was spent waiting for something to happen. The first requirement, therefore, is to create an atmosphere of tension prior to the battle scenes. It is for each reader to decide whether they feel this has been achieved. If so, how was it done; what was it that made you feel tense. If not, what do you feel was lacking?

- Sebastian Faulks has chosen to portray the battle and its consequences very graphically, but also very poetically. His description of the Battle of the Somme is both brutal and lyrical. The poetry of Wilfred Owen (especially *Dulce et Decorum Est*) or Isaac Rosenberg (*Dead Man's Dump*) reinforces how well this contrast can work.

- The letters which the men send prior to the battle show the personal side of warfare, demonstrating each man's thoughts and reminding us how much they have to lose. This hits the reader much harder when many of the letter-writers later die.

- Another narrative tool, namely Elizabeth Benson's personal journey to discover more about her ancestry, reveals some of the statistics and facts behind the battle. Her visit to Thiepval, for instance, serves as a reminder to the reader that so many lives were lost during the battle which has just been described.

- Other authors have dealt with this subject, including Erich Maria Remarque in *All Quiet on the Western Front*. Students could also read some of the memoirs of the First World War to discover how the real combatants recalled their own experiences. These could include *General Jack's Diary*, edited by John Terraine or *The Last of the Ebb* by Sidney Rogerson, among many others.

Additional information and guidance on this topic, both in *Birdsong* and other novels, can be found in this Study Guide, in the Chapter entitled *Themes and Comparisons - The Depiction of Battle Scenes*.

(d) 'Explain how the structure of the novel *Birdsong* affects the reader's interpretation.'

- Firstly you need to decide whether, and to what extent, the structure of the novel has impacted on your interpretation. If the answer is 'It hasn't', then this clearly is not the task for you! If, however, you feel that Part One is an irrelevant sexual romp, or that the modern sections serve no purpose, or equally, that all seven parts are required in order for the whole piece to work, you could consider this as a topic.

- Whichever viewpoint you take, this must reflect your own feelings about the novel. It is no use repeating something which you have read somewhere else as you will not be able to conclusively argue your point.

- If you decide that Part One is unnecessary, you must give a reasoned argument as to why. Is this because you feel that it has no impact on the main point of the novel? If so, then what is the main point of the novel? Is it meant just to be a study of war; or is it really an examination of people?

- If, on the other hand, you can find no purpose for the modern sections of the book, think about why you feel like this. Remember that their purpose is, essentially, to inform. This is really a narrative tool, employed by Sebastian Faulks to fill in the gaps. Do you feel that this works, and if not, what else could Faulks have done to perform the same task?

- Those who feel that the whole structure works perfectly could examine why others (and there are many others), disagree. Why, for example, do you think that some people dislike Part One and/or the modern sections of the novel? And what makes them work for you?

- Reasoned arguments are required. You cannot simply say 'I like/hate this because...'. You must, instead, decide upon how you feel about the novel's structure and whether you believe it works. Then evaluate why you have reacted in the way that you have. You must assess *how* Faulks has created that reaction, rather than just your reaction itself.

Additional information and guidance on this topic can be found in this Study Guide, in the Chapter entitled *Critical Analysis - The Structure of the Novel*.

Other possible topics...

- Students could choose to explore Faulks's use of **language**, possibly making comparisons between his portrayal of battle scenes, wounds and death with his descriptions of sexual intercourse and birth, focusing on the impact of these narratives on the reader.

- The representation of the **home front**, although not featured heavily in *Birdsong*, is nonetheless, represented. However, Faulks gives just one, unfavourable perspective. Students could, therefore choose to examine this, discussing its authenticity and how others have treated this topic.

- An examination of the portrayal of **faith** within the novel could be chosen, with students exploring the importance of faith to the characters involved and whether - or how - their beliefs change as the story unfolds. The context and authenticity of these portrayals should also be explained.

CREATIVE TRANSFORMATIONAL WRITING

As the title suggests, this option gives the student more scope for creativity - within certain limitations. Here, rather than writing a piece which clinically analyses one or more aspects of the novel, you could choose to become the author instead. Do not be fooled into thinking that this provides you with an 'easy' option, however. Your essay MUST demonstrate that you have understood not only the content, language, structure and narrative viewpoint of the novel, but also that you have completely absorbed the author's style and purpose in writing it in the first place.

Within the restrictions of the permitted word-count and the fact that the assessment objectives remain the same, you have to adopt the style - both narrative and linguistic - of Sebastian Faulks, retain the characterisations which he has already created, focus on the context of the novel and make your piece believable and realistic.

There are several possibilities within this choice of essay:

(a) Stephen's Notebook

- You could take one episode in Stephen's life and re-create a relevant notebook entry. Possible examples for topics might include:
  - Stephen's war-time meeting with Isabelle;
  - Hearing the news of Weir's death;
  - Recovering from the wounds received in the tunnel;
  - Any of the battle/death/wounding scenes in which Stephen is involved;
  - Stephen's feelings upon returning to England on leave;
  - The episode with the prostitute.

- Remember that you must write in the style of Sebastian Faulks, but that you are writing from Stephen's perspective. The language and tone must reflect this. Use the notebook extract provided at the end of Part Five, although remember that by the time he wrote this, Stephen's character had become disillusioned and war-weary. Your piece should demonstrate your interpretation of his state of mind at the time of writing.

- You should include and refer to, but not repeat verbatim, the episode(s) as referred to in the text. Make yourself extremely familiar with the events you have chosen to describe, so that you cannot miss anything out, but also remember not to include scenes or experiences which Stephen has not witnessed himself. You may, of course, allow him to refer to incidents about which he has later been informed, taking care as to how these are introduced and bearing in mind that Stephen's character is unlikely to 'gossip'.

- Relate Stephen's feelings and reactions to his past and his previous experiences. This helps to demonstrate your understanding, not only of the particular circumstances which form your topic, but of the whole novel and, especially, characters involved.

- Read other memoirs or narratives of the First World War, especially those that may relate directly to the events you have chosen to describe. These will help you to understand how much detail is required. However, be careful to stick to the style of Faulks, rather than adopting that of any of the other writers. Possible texts to study could include *Undertones of War* by Edmund Blunden or *Somme* by Lyn MacDonald.

Additional information and guidance on this topic can be found in this Study Guide, in the Chapter entitled *Character Analysis - Stephen Wraysford*.

(b) The missing years

- You could choose to write an account of Stephen's two years of silence following the end of the war.

- We know that Stephen and Jeanne were married in 1919 and went to live in Norfolk with Françoise. Use this information as a basis to write an essay explaining what happened to the family and how, eventually, Stephen began to speak again.

- Explore Stephen's likely reactions to the news of Isabelle's death and the discovery that he has a daughter. Use Françoise's brief accounts to help understand her perspective of her father.

- Remember that you are acting as a third-person narrator. In the case of *Birdsong*, the narrator has a certain amount of insight into the thoughts and feelings of the characters. You could, however, use letters to enhance this.

Additional information and guidance on this topic can be found in this Study Guide, in the Chapter entitled *Character Analysis - Stephen Wraysford* and *Jeanne Fourmentier*

(c) Letters

- Correspondence between various characters form a part of the narrative structure, serving the purpose of explaining events or reactions, from the sole perspective of the writer of each letter. Within this topic, you have several options available:

- A letter, written in Munich, from Isabelle to Jeanne (found by Elizabeth amongst Françoise's possessions), explaining her actions in following Max to live in Germany. You could, perhaps, explore Isabelle's feelings for Stephen, compared with her stronger emotional link to Max. You might also hint at the beginnings of the influenza which would eventually claim Isabelle's life, and her request that Jeanne should bring up Françoise in her absence.

- An imaginary letter, written from Isabelle to Stephen, explaining her departure in 1910. We know that Isabelle began to write such a letter, but found it impossible to explain her actions. Using your knowledge of Isabelle's character you could try to write a feasible explanation of her decision, remembering that you must not reveal the fact that Isabelle is pregnant.

- Imagining that, following his rescue from the tunnel, Stephen has been sent to recuperate, you could write a letter to him from Jeanne. In this, she might explain her love for him; her hopes for their future, offering him encouragement in his recovery. She might also make the suggestion of marriage - being as she is the stronger of the two characters at this stage, why should the proposal not come from her? It would also be in character for Jeanne to propose in writing, rather than in person and might take the form of her suggesting that she could nurse him, but that she understands he might prefer to live in England, away from the memories of Isabelle and the war.

- Whatever your choice of character and letter, remember to write the correspondence from their perspective. You are not narrating this essay, but are representing a specific character. Read the other letters in the novel and use them to help create your own.

- Keep to context in your letter. Remember the timeline of events and do not deviate, but also retain a wartime feel. So, for example, although Jeanne may have shared Stephen's joke that they will 'shock the whole of Rouen' by living together, does this really strike you as something which Jeanne would find acceptable? This is not only dictated by Jeanne's character but also by the time and place in which she lived.

- You may be able to demonstrate a deeper knowledge of the text by referring to unknown reactions to events. You could create these reactions or thoughts using your understanding of the character(s) involved.

Additional information and guidance on this topic can be found in this Study Guide, in the Chapter entitled *Character Analysis*.

2. COMPARATIVE WORK

Students can choose to compare, or connect, their chosen prose text with their preferred drama piece. This is only one of the options available and students may prefer to restrict their comparative piece to plays only. In my opinion, *Birdsong* would not be my first choice of text to use, when comparing or contrasting with any of the set plays. I have, therefore, limited the suggestions to *Journey's End* and *The Accrington Pals*, as *Not About Heroes* does not, in my view, provide sufficient suitable material to compare or contrast with *Birdsong* as a text. Students should bear in mind that *Birdsong* is a novel, intended to be read, while the plays are intended to be performed, generally, before a live audience. This makes a difference in the suitability of some content. If you have chosen to use *Birdsong* as your prose text and wish to use it for comparative purposes, there are a few options as to how this could be achieved.

JOURNEY'S END and BIRDSONG

These two texts probably form the most obvious choices for comparison, in that they have several common themes which the authors have treated differently. Comparing setting, structure and language is more difficult in this case as *Birdsong* does not really lend itself to such a task. I have, therefore, focused on themes and characters.

THEME AND CHARACTER BASED COURSEWORK

Students have several options here, and could look at any of the following themes, focusing (where appropriate) on the portrayal of the characters involved:

Male Relationships

Here students could look at the element of **hero-worship** and relate it to the relationships between Raleigh and Stanhope in *Journey's End*, and Weir and Wraysford in *Birdsong*. Bear in mind that the two sets of men meet in different circumstances: in one case their friendship pre-existed the war. This would, naturally, have a great effect on the perception of each other. Weir's dependence on Stephen increases throughout the novel, but the same cannot be said of Raleigh, who matures quickly once he has entered the dugout and witnessed the impact of the war on his old friend, Stanhope.

Alternatively, students could focus on the **relationships between officers and men**. Stanhope is portrayed, right from the beginning of the play, as a considerate officer, always concerned for his men, despite his own problems. Wraysford, on the other hand, is shown to be more self-centred at the beginning of the novel. He cannot bring himself to care about the men under his charge and wonders at their perseverance. Gradually he begins to change and eventually, his men do seem to become of greater importance. Students would need to examine how the two authors have portrayed this element, bearing in mind that Sherriff was an officer during the First World War.

Portrayal of Fear
Both authors have included characters who show a fear of their situation, showing the different ways in which they manage to control this. In *Journey's End*, Hibbert is clearly terrified of spending any time in the trenches and dreads the anticipated attack. Sherriff portrays his character unfavourably, making the reader less concerned for his safety or feelings. Other characters in the play are also fearful, but they control their emotions better. In *Birdsong*, there are several examples of men demonstrating fear. Tipper has a complete physical breakdown due to his dread of battle, but he overcomes this and returns to the trenches. Stephen's fear becomes greater as the novel progresses. Every time he is away from the front, he dreads returning. This growing, increasing fear might have been used to show a breakdown, but instead, Stephen seems to rise above it. Students could choose to look at the portrayal of these characters and the reasons why they have been given the traits they have.

Futility
A particularly common theme in the novels and plays of the First World War, this aspect is portrayed in *Birdsong*, by the graphic descriptions of the waste

of lives on the battlefields, in conjunction with Stephen's desperate need to understand the situation - which, of course, he never does. In *Journey's End*, there are many circumstances where this theme is portrayed. One of the main ones is the death of Osborne - probably one of the most likeable characters in the play, and certainly the most useful. His death, on a raid, gains nothing, but the cost to Stanhope and the other officers, is beyond comparison. The two authors have used different methods of portraying this. Faulks has, occasionally, given Stephen's character the opportunity, either in thought, word or letters, to moralise as to the conduct of the war, frequently expressing views which offer a negative opinion. One example of this is Stephen's letter to Isabelle, written on the eve of the Battle of the Somme. Sherriff, on the other hand, is more subtle and none of the characters make great statements about the war in general.

Stanhope and Wraysford

A slightly different task, students could choose to focus directly on the portrayal of two characters, one from each text. This would only really work with Stanhope and Wraysford, as they are, effectively, the two 'leads' and make an obvious choice for comparison. They both suffer greatly from the effects of war-fatigue; both turn to alcohol. The reader (or audience) learn of Stanhope's deterioration through other characters. Osborne defends Stanhope's actions to Hardy in the first scene, while Raleigh paints and glorified image of his former schoolboy hero, which we then discover is no longer the case. In *Birdsong*, we witness Stephen's deterioration as the novel progresses, as Faulks slowly builds towards his breakdown. It is only afterwards that we learn that following the end of the conflict, he did not speak for two years, showing that the impact of his experiences was greater than we had been led to believe.

THE ACCRINGTON PALS and BIRDSONG

Again, I have based the following suggestions on themes and characters within these two texts.

THEME AND CHARACTER BASED COURSEWORK

There are several possible themes which students could choose to study in this section of their coursework studies, most of which also incorporate an in-depth analysis of the characters involved.

The Home Front

The Accrington Pals is set, almost entirely, on the home front, examining the effects of the war on a small group of working-class people - mainly women. The attitudes of the characters towards the conflict vary greatly and, in many cases, change after the men have gone away to fight. In this play, the audience - or reader - witnesses the impact of the loss of almost all of the young men in the town. Sebastian Faulks has given us one interpretation of the home front throughout his novel - namely that civilians are callous and unthinking, concerned mainly with their own problems and hardships. Birdsong, although it has an omniscient narrator, and is written in the third-person, is told essentially from the soldier's perspective. This gives it a bias towards their point of view. So, we are not told how Weir's parents really feel, or how they behave when he is not present. We are only given Weir's version of events and his reaction to them. Due to the fact that The Accrington Pals is a play, each character offers a different response to their situation and the audience is able to interpret this through the actor's performance. This greatly affects the understanding of the author's portrayal.

The Portrayal of Relationships

There are several romantic attachments portrayed in The Accrington Pals, most of which are treated differently. May and Tom have a very awkward relationship, made more so by their differing opinions on almost everything. In addition, May does not support Tom's decision to enlist and her affections for him are constantly tested. Tom, on the other hand, knows exactly how he feels about May, but also wants to do his duty. Other relationships include the ones between Ralph and Eva and Arthur and Annie Boggis, both of which are more stereotypical. Birdsong gives us less scope for study, but students could still look at the relationship forged between Jeanne and Stephen. Jeanne is the stronger of these two characters (similar to May Hassal in The Accrington Pals), but this is because Stephen has already been so worn down by the war. Stephen is also still in love with Isabelle, Jeanne's sister, which adds an element of guilt to her side of their growing affections. In The Accrington Pals, many of the women are portrayed as quite harsh and some even seem glad when their men-folk leave for war. However, this is contrasted with their reactions to the news that so many have been killed in the Battle of the Somme. Students could also look at how sex has been portrayed within these relationships. For Stephen and Jeanne, there is no mention of sex: the war and Isabelle's abandonment have left Stephen a broken man. Jeanne must first mend him, before their relationship even has a chance of becoming physical. In The Accrington Pals, Peter Whelan gives us two different portrayals of sex. Firstly there is the relationship between Ralph and Eva, which is physical, although their sexual intercourse is, for obvious reasons, conducted behind closed doors. May and Tom never have sex, although it is something they both consider. Bearing in mind that these two pieces were written in the latter part of the twentieth century, the portrayals of attitudes towards sex are remarkably different.

Religion or Faith
Both The Accrington Pals and Birdsong feature characters who have a belief in God, which they try to uphold. Both Arthur Boggis and Jack Firebrace have a strong faith, but eventually both of them come to question their beliefs. Jack Firebrace's character faces the loss of his beloved son, but still maintains his belief in the goodness of his God. He writes to his wife, explaining his belief that, despite their loss, they should be grateful to God for John's existence and presence in their lives. It is only when he witnesses the carnage on the battlefields of the Somme, that he begins to doubt. Arthur Boggis's speeches are invariably littered with references to his religious beliefs; he writes to his friend, explaining that he believes he is doing God's work. Once Arthur is at the front, his attitude changes and, before his death, he denounces his God, wondering at how He could allow such suffering to take place. Both authors treat this subject in a similar fashion - even using letters to explain the characters' reactions. Both characters are working-class and from similar

backgrounds and both are married. By contrast, Stephen Wraysford's character, while not becoming overtly religious, seems to gain a kind of faith during the course of the novel. As a young man, Stephen is portrayed as someone with no beliefs in anything but himself, and then his love for Isabelle. Gradually he gains a sense of humanity and consideration for others. Students should bear in mind that at the time of the First World War, religion was of significant importance to many people and the attendance of religious services prior to battles, as portrayed in *Birdsong*, was commonplace.

FURTHER READING RECOMMENDATIONS FOR STUDENTS

Students are often expected to demonstrate a sound knowledge of the texts which they are studying and also to enhance this knowledge with extensive reading of other books within this genre. I have provided on the following pages a list of books, poetry, plays and non-fiction which, in my opinion, provide a good basic understanding of this topic. In addition, a small review of each book has been provided to help students choose which of the following are most suitable for them. Those marked with an 'A' are, in my opinion, suitable only for students of A-Level and above.

NOVELS

STRANGE MEETING by Susan Hill

Strange Meeting is a beautiful and moving book. It is the story of two young men, who meet in the worst circumstances, yet manage to overcome their surroundings and form a deep and lasting friendship. They are opposites: John Hilliard is quiet and reserved, while David Barton is outgoing and friendly. Despite their differences, their friendship blossoms, as the world around them disintegrates into self-destruction. Susan Hill writes so evocatively that the reader is automatically drawn into the lives of these men: the sights, sounds and even smells which they witness are brought to life. This is a book about war and its effects; it is also a story of love, both conventional and 'forbidden'; of human relationships of every variety. This is a tale told during the worst of times, about the best of men and is, quite simply, one of the best novels ever written about the First World War.

A VERY LONG ENGAGEMENT by Sebastien Japrisot

A story of enduring love, truth and determination. Refusing to believe that her fiancé can possibly have left her forever, Mathilde decides to search for Manech whom she has been told is missing, presumed dead. She learns from a first-hand witness, that he may not have died, so she sets out on a voyage of discovery - learning not just about his fate, but also a great deal about herself and human nature. Mathilde herself has to overcome her own personal fears and hardships and, out of sheer persistence and a refusal to accept the obvious, she eventually discovers the truth. Although this novel does not form part of the main syllabus reading list, it does make an interesting and fairly easy read and is useful from the perspective that it gives a French woman's viewpoint of the war.

REGENERATION by Pat Barker

This book is, as its title implies, a novel about the rebuilding of men following extreme trauma. Billy Prior is a young working-class officer - a 'temporary gentleman' - who finds himself at Craiglockhart Military Hospital in Edinburgh, having been damaged by his experiences on the Western Front. It is the job of Dr W. H. R. Rivers, to 'mend' Prior, and others like him, ready for them to return to the fighting, while wrestling with his own conscience at the same time. Interweaved into this central plot is the meeting, also at Craiglockhart, of poets Siegfried Sassoon and Wilfred Owen, who are both there to receive treatment. This mixture of fact and fiction within a novel has created some controversy, but it is a common feature within this genre and one which Pat Barker handles better than most. This is an immensely useful book - even if not read as part of the Trilogy - as it takes place away from the front lines, showing the reader the deep and long-lasting effects of battle upon men, whose lives would never be the same again. Due to some adult content, we recommend this book for A-Level students only.

THE RETURN OF THE SOLDIER by Rebecca West

Written in 1918, by an author who had lived through the conflict, this home-front novel gives a useful insight into the trauma of war and society's reaction, as seen through the eyes of three women. Chris Baldry, an officer and husband of Kitty, returns home mid-way through the war, suffering from shell-shock and amnesia. He believes that that he is still in a relationship with Margaret Allington - his first love from fifteen years earlier. Kitty, Margaret and Chris's cousin, Jenny, must decide whether to leave Chris in his make-believe world, safe from the war; or whether to 'cure' him and risk his future welfare once he returns to being a soldier. A useful novel from many perspectives in that it was written right at the end of the war, and it gives a female, home-front view of the effects of the war on individuals and families.

ALL QUIET ON THE WESTERN FRONT by Erich Maria Remarque

Written from first-hand experience of life in the trenches, this novel is the moving account of the lives of a group of young German soldiers during the First World War. Remarque had been in the trenches during the later stages of the war and this poignant account of war is a must-read for all those who show an interest in this subject. His descriptions of trench-life and battles are second-to-none and his portrayal of the close friendships forged between the men make this an immensely valuable piece of literature. The fact that this, often shocking, story is told from a German perspective also demonstrates the universal horrors of the war and the sympathy between men of both sides for others enduring the same hardships as themselves.

A LONG LONG WAY by Sebastian Barry

Sebastian Barry's novel tells the a story of Willie Dunne, a young Irish volunteer serving in the trenches of the Western Front. Willie must not only contend with the horrors of the war, but also his own confused feelings regarding the Easter uprising of 1916, and his father's disapproval. Willie's feelings and doubts lead to great upheavals in his life, including personal losses and betrayals by those whom he had believed he could trust. This is an interesting novel about loyalty, war and love, although it does suffer from a degree of historical inaccuracy. In our opinion, due to the adult content of this novel, it is suitable only for A-Level students.

NOT SO QUIET… by Helen Zenna Smith

This novel describes the lives of women working very close to the front line on the Western Front during the First World War, as ambulance drivers. Theirs is a dangerous job, in harsh conditions, with little or no respite. Helen (or Smithy, as she is called by her friends), eventually breaks down under the pressure of the work and returns, briefly, to England. An excellent novel for studying the female perspective, as well as the home front.

POETRY

It is recommended that students read from a wide variety of poets, including female writers. The following anthologies provide good resources for students.

POEMS OF THE FIRST WORLD WAR - NEVER SUCH INNOCENCE
Edited by Martin Stephen

Probably one of the finest anthologies of First World War poetry currently available. Martin Stephen has collected together some of the best known works by some of the most famous and well-read poets and mixed these with more obscure verses, including many by women and those on the home-front, together with some popular songs both from home and from the front. These have been interspersed with excellent notes which give the reader sufficient information without being too weighty. At the back of the book, there are short biographical notes on many of the poets. This is a fine anthology, suitable both for those who are starting out with their studies, and for the more experienced reader.

LADS: LOVE POETRY OF THE TRENCHES by Martin Taylor

Featuring many lesser-known poets and poems, this anthology approaches the First World War from a different perspective: love. A valuable introduction discusses the emotions of men who, perhaps for the first time, were discovering their own capacity to love their fellow man. This is not an anthology of purely homo-erotic poems, but also features verses by those who had found affection and deep, lasting friendship in the trenches of the First World War.

SCARS UPON MY HEART
Selected by Catherine Reilly

First published in 1981, this anthology is invaluable as it features a collection of poems written exclusively by women on the subject of the First World War. Some of the better known female poets are featured here, such as Vera Brittain and Jessie Pope, but there are also many more writers who are less famous. In addition there are some poets whose work is featured, who are not now renowned for their poetry, but for their works in other areas of literature. Many of the poets included here have minor biographical details featured at the end of the anthology. This book has become the 'standard' for those wishing to study the female contribution to this genre.

UP THE LINE TO DEATH
Edited by Brian Gardner

This anthology, described by its editor Brian Gardner as a 'book about war', is probably, and deservedly, one of the most widely read in this genre. The famous and not-so-famous sit happily together within in these pages of carefully selected poetry. Arranged thematically, these poems provide a poet's-eye-view of the progression of the war, from the initial euphoria and nationalistic pride of John Freeman's 'Happy is England Now' to Sassoon's plea that we should 'never forget'. Useful biographical details and introductions complete this book, which is almost certainly the most useful and important of all the First World War poetry anthologies.

NON-FICTION

UNDERTONES OF WAR by Edmund Blunden

Edmund Blunden's memoir of his experiences in the First World War is a moving, enlightening and occasionally humorous book, demonstrating above all the intense feelings of respect and comradeship which Blunden found in the trenches.

MEMOIRS OF AN INFANTRY OFFICER by Siegfried Sassoon

Following on from *Memoirs of a Fox-hunting Man*, this book is an
autobiographical account of Sassoon's life during the First World War.
Sassoon has changed the names of the characters and George Sherston
(Sassoon) is not a poet. Sassoon became one of the war's most famous poets
and this prose account of his war provides useful background information.
(For a list of the fictional characters and their factual counterparts, see
Appendix II of *Siegfried Sassoon* by John Stuart Roberts.)

THE GREAT WAR GENERALS ON THE WESTERN FRONT 1914-1918 by Robin Neillands

Like many others before and since, the cover of this book claims that it will
dismiss the old myth that the troops who served in the First World War were
badly served by their senior officers. Unlike most of the other books,
however, this one is balanced and thought-provoking. Of particular interest
within this book is the final chapter which provides an assessment of the
main protagonists and their role in the conflict.

THE WESTERN FRONT by Richard Holmes

This is one of many history books about the First World War. Dealing
specifically with the Western Front, Richard Holmes looks at the creation of
the trench warfare system, supplying men and munitions, major battles and
living on the front line..

LETTERS FROM A LOST GENERATION (FIRST WORLD WAR LETTERS OF VERA BRITTAIN AND FOUR FRIENDS) Edited by Alan Bishop and Mark Bostridge

A remarkable insight into the changes which the First World War caused to a
particular set of individuals. In this instance, Vera Brittain lost four important
people in her life (two close friends, her fiancé and her brother). The agony
this evoked is demonstrated through letters sent between these five
characters, which went on to form the basis of Vera Brittain's autobiography
Testament of Youth.

1914-1918: VOICES AND IMAGES OF THE GREAT WAR
by Lyn MacDonald

One of the most useful 'unofficial' history books available to those studying the First World War. This book tells the story of the soldiers who fought the war through their letters, diary extracts, newspaper reports, poetry and eye-witness accounts. As with all of Lyn MacDonald's excellent books, *Voices and Images of the Great War* tells its story through the words of the people who were there. The author gives just the right amount of background information of a political and historical nature to keep the reader interested and informed, while leaving the centre-stage to those who really matter... the men themselves.

BIBLIOGRAPHY

BIRDSONG by Sebastian Faulks

ALL QUIET ON THE WESTERN FRONT by Erich Maria Remarque

THE RETURN OF THE SOLDIER by Rebecca West

JOURNEY'S END by R C Sherriff

REGENERATION by Pat Barker

THE EYE IN THE DOOR by Pat Barker

THE GHOST ROAD by Pat Barker

STRANGE MEETING by Susan Hill

A LONG LONG WAY by Sebastian Barry

UNDERTONES OF WAR by Edmund Blunden

SIEGFRIED'S JOURNEY by Siegfried Sassoon

MEMOIRS OF AN INFANTRY OFFICER by Siegfried Sassoon

TWELVE DAYS ON THE SOMME by Sidney Rogerson

THE LAST OF THE EBB by Sidney Rogerson

GENERAL JACK'S DIARY edited by John Terraine

ALL QUIET ON THE HOME FRONT by Richard Van Emden and Steve Humphries

UP THE LINE TO DEATH by Brian Gardner

OTHER GREAT WAR LITERATURE STUDY GUIDE TITLES

GREAT WAR LITERATURE STUDY GUIDE PAPERBACKS:

Title	ISBN
A Long Long Way A-Level Study Guide	978-1905378401
All Quiet on the Western Front	978-1905378302
Journey's End - GCSE	978-1905378371
Journey's End - A-Level	978-1905378401
Regeneration A-Level Study Guide	978-1905378395
Strange Meeting A-Level Study Guide	978-1905378456
The Return of the Soldier	978-1905378357
Female Poets of the First World War - Vol.1	978-1905378258
War Poets of the First World War - Vol.1	978-1905378241
War Poets of the First World War - Vol.2	978-1905378425
First World War Plays	978-1905378418

GREAT WAR LITERATURE STUDY GUIDE E-BOOKS:

NOVELS & PLAYS

A Long Long Way
All Quiet on the Western Front
Journey's End (A-Level or GCSE)
Regeneration
Strange Meeting
The Return of the Soldier
The Accrington Pals
Not About Heroes
Oh What a Lovely War

POET BIOGRAPHIES AND POETRY ANALYSIS:

Harold Begbie
Edmund Blunden
Rupert Brooke
May Wedderburn Cannan
Margaret Postgate Cole
Nancy Cunard
Eleanor Farjeon
Gilbert Frankau
Wilfrid Wilson Gibson
Robert Graves
Julian Grenfell
Ivor Gurney
Alan P Herbert
W N Hodgson
Geoffrey Anketell Studdert Kennedy
E A Mackintosh
John McCrae
Charlotte Mew
Edith Nesbit
Robert Nichols

Wilfred Owen
Jessie Pope
Isaac Rosenberg
Siegfried Sassoon
Charles Hamilton Sorley
Edward Wyndham Tennant
Edward Thomas
Iris Tree
Katharine Tynan Hinkson
Robert Ernest Vernède
Arthur Graeme West

Please note that e-books are only available direct from our Web site at www.greatwarliterature.co.uk and cannot be purchased through bookshops.